DREAM ANALYSIS
IN PSYCHOTHERAPY

Pergamon Titles of Related Interest

Anchin/Kiesler HANDBOOK OF INTERPERSONAL
PSYCHOTHERAPY
Hersen/Kazdin/Bellack THE CLINICAL PSYCHOLOGY
HANDBOOK
Nietzel/Dillehay PSYCHOLOGICAL CONSULTATION IN THE
COURTROOM
Romanczyk CLINICAL UTILIZATION OF MICROCOMPUTER
TECHNOLOGY

Related Journals

(Free sample copies available upon request)

CLINICAL PSYCHOLOGY REVIEW
COMPUTERS IN HUMAN BEHAVIOR

PSYCHOLOGY PRACTITIONER GUIDEBOOKS

EDITORS

Arnold P. Goldstein, Syracuse University
Leonard Krasner, SUNY at Stony Brook
Sol L. Garfield, Washington University

DREAM ANALYSIS IN PSYCHOTHERAPY

LILLIE WEISS
Center for Psychotherapy and Dream Analysis
and Arizona State University

PERGAMON PRESS
New York   Oxford   Toronto   Sydney   Frankfurt

Pergamon Press Offices:

U.S.A.	Pergamon Press Inc., Maxwell House, Fairview Park, Elmsford, New York 10523, U.S.A.
U.K.	Pergamon Press Ltd., Headington Hill Hall, Oxford OX3 0BW, England
CANADA	Pergamon Press Canada Ltd., Suite 104, 150 Consumers Road, Willowdale, Ontario M2J 1P9, Canada
AUSTRALIA	Pergamon Press (Aust.) Pty. Ltd., P.O. Box 544, Potts Point, NSW 2011, Australia
FEDERAL REPUBLIC OF GERMANY	Pergamon Press GmbH, Hammerweg 6, D-6242 Kronberg-Taunus, Federal Republic of Germany
BRAZIL	Pergamon Editora Ltda., Rua Eça de Queiros, 346, CEP 04011, São Paulo, Brazil
JAPAN	Pergamon Press Ltd., 8th Floor, Matsuoka Central Building, 1-7-1 Nishishinjuku, Shinjuku, Tokyo 160, Japan
PEOPLE'S REPUBLIC OF CHINA	Pergamon Press, Qianmen Hotel, Beijing, People's Republic of China

---

First printing 1986

Library of Congress Cataloging in Publication Data

Weiss, Lillie.
    Dream analysis in psychotherapy.

    (Psychology practitioner guidebook)
    1. Dreams--Therapeutic use. 2. Psychoanalysis.
3. Psychotherapy. I. Title. II. Series.
RC489.D74W45   1986   616.89'14   85-26040
ISBN 0-08-033162-9
ISBN 0-08-033161-0 (pbk.)

Printed in the United States of America

Contents

Preface

Florida, October 10, 1980

I was sitting in Hattie Rosenthal's study during an intensive training session. I recounted the following dream:

We are about to play a game. I very excitedly take out the money for it—five dollars in all—four bills and one dollar in change. I don't remember the whole dream, but my feeling is one of excitement, almost as though I am cheating, like I already know I have good cards in my hands, and I am excited about being able to gamble.

"Whom were you playing with?"

"I'm not really sure. I think it was some children I used to play cards with when I was a little girl."

"What makes you so certain you will win?"

"I don't know. I think I have good cards in my hands."

"Why do you feel you are cheating?"

"I guess because I am playing with kids. It's not really fair. I have an advantage when I play with children."

"What is a game?"

"It's where someone wins or loses, like life."

"Why would an adult woman play with children? And for money too!"

"I don't know." I was beginning to get uncomfortable.

"Just take a guess. Why do you suppose a grown-up, not yourself, would play with children instead of with adults?"

"I guess she may fear competition. She may be afraid to take a risk. She may lose or fail."

"And why do you think someone would be so afraid of failure?"

I was getting more and more uncomfortable. Hattie smiled and answered for me: "Because she wants to be an unfailing person!"

We laughed together. Regardless of content, my dreams usually had the same theme. Hattie continued, "You know what I always say: 'To try and fail is to succeed. Not to try is failure.'" There was Hattie, as always, encouraging me to risk, not to be afraid. "And what is money? You take out five dollars."

"It is something to get what you want."

"What are five energies or abilities you have that help you get what you want in life?" I listed five attributes.

"Four bills and one in change: Four you are sure of—one you are not. Which one of your abilities do you doubt?"

Details, details, always paying attention to each detail. That was Hattie, never letting anything go in a dream, reminding me that every aspect of a dream is important; otherwise we would not dream it.

Dr. Hattie Rosenthal was born in Germany in 1894 and came to the United States following World War II. She received her training from Freida Fromm-Reichman, a leading psychoanalyst. Dr. Rosenthal was President of the Hattie R. Rosenthal Institute in Florida and had been active in writing, teaching, and interpreting dreams for many decades. Her autobiography, *Against All Odds* (1978a), describes the uniqueness of this individual. Her many years of experience, her inner wisdom, and her skills have contributed to her developing a unique approach to the interpretation of dream in psychotherapy. Her techniques clarify and simplify the translation of dreams into invaluable information for the psychotherapist. Rosenthal's approach to dream analysis helps in quickly reaching the core issues in psychotherapy, thereby shortening the psychotherapeutic process. Dr. Rosenthal published several articles and monographs on her work. She died on April 11, 1983, at the age of 89 before her main manuscript in this area was published.

The theory and guidelines in this book are based on Dr. Rosenthal's work. Although her training was primarily psychoanalytic, this book adapts her method of interpretation to make it compatible with a number of theoretical orientations. This book is for the clinician, regardless of theoretical orientation, who would like to learn new skills and make more use of dream interpretation in work with clients.

The book is divided into two parts. The first part is an introduction to dream analysis. These chapters provide a historical and research overview and describe the use of dreams in psychotherapy, the theory of dream analysis, and how to present it to a client. The second part discusses the interpretive process in step-by-step fashion. Each chapter in this section is devoted to a detailed analysis of each of the steps used in interpreting a dream, together with clinical examples. The last chapter summarizes and integrates all of the steps and presents some guidelines for the clinician.

This book is dedicated to Hattie Rosenthal whom I have had the good fortune to have had as therapist, friend, mentor, and guide, for giving me the courage to take risks and "stop playing with children."

Acknowledgments

I would like to thank all of the people who have shared their dreams with me. They have taught me a great deal and made it possible for me to write this book. I am also indebted to Jerome Frank, Angela Piliouras, and the rest of the staff at Pergamon Press for their help and suggestions. Special thanks go to Sandra McDill for her hard work in typing the manuscript as well as to my husband and friends for their encouragement.

Chapter 1
Historical Background

This chapter provides a historical perspective on the use of dreams in psychotherapy. Psychological as well as nonpsychological views of dreaming will be presented. Various theories and methods will be described, and some recent clinical applications of dreams will be reviewed.

PSYCHOLOGICAL THEORIES
OF DREAMING

Although the use of dreams dates back to ancient times, it was not until Sigmund Freud published his study *The Interpretation of Dreams* in 1899 that dreams were viewed as important in modern medicine. Before Freud developed his theory of the dream process, medicine considered dreams as meaningless hallucinations. By studying his own dreams at length, Freud developed a theory of dreams that has been one of the major influences in psychotherapy over the past few decades. Almost all dream theories derive from it, even when they take issue with it.

According to Freud, dreams were disguised wishes of infantile sexual needs. He emphasized the wish fulfillment function of dreams, stating, "When the work of interpretation is completed, the dream can be recognized as a wish-fulfillment" (Freud, 1950, p. 32). Freud distinguished between the *manifest dream*, the dream that one recalls, and the *latent dream*, which is its underlying meaning. The manifest dream was disguised so that its content would not shock the dreamer into awakening. The latent content is disguised by certain processes, such as condensation, displacement, secondary elaboration, dramatization, and symbolism. Freud gave examples of these dream mechanisms, which he termed "the dream work," and discussed how these served to disguise the latent meaning of the dream. For example, in condensation, several latent dream ideas are condensed into a single image in the dream recalled. In displacement, the affect connected with a specific object is transferred to another in order to distract the dreamer's attention from the real object of his or her feelings. Secondary elaboration is the unconscious revision of the dream as it is recalled, again to disguise the underlying wish. Dramatization is the presentation of thoughts in a dramatic, exaggerated form. Symbolization is another mechanism that serves a disguise function. Freud viewed almost all objects and activities in dreams as sexual symbols, believing that symbols in dreams were primarily representations of male or female genitals.

Freud viewed dreams as the royal road to the unconscious, where the repressed, hidden impulses that were unacceptable to conscious thought were buried. His method of interpretation for arriving at the latent dream content was to have the patient associate to every element in the manifest dream. This was the method of free association that he used in psycho-analysis to lead back to the dream's latent, disguised meaning. He de-scribed his method as follows:

> The patient should take up a restful position and close his eyes; he must be explicitly instructed to renounce all criticism of the thought formations which he may perceive. He must also be told that the success of the psychoanalysis depends upon his noting and communicating everything that passes through his mind, and that he must not allow himself to sup-press one idea because it seems to him unimportant or irrelevant to the sub-ject, or another because it seems nonsensical. (Freud, 1950, p. 13)

The free-floating associations that patients make through this method help them arrive at the dream's underlying meaning.

The disguise function of dreams not only allows the dreamer to discharge forbidden wishes, but also allows the dreamer to sleep undis-turbed by concealing the nature of the wish. Freud saw the dream as func-tioning both as a guardian of sleep and as a safety valve for unacceptable wishes. The sleep-protection and safety-valve functions of dreams were offered by Freud almost as afterthoughts and were developed before knowledge of the scientific experiments of sleep and dreams. Jones (1968) distinguishes between the psychoanalytic theory of dreaming and the psychoanalytic theory of dreams. The former concerns the processes of *dream formation*, whereas the latter concerns *dream interpretation*. It is the latter theory that deals with the uses of dreams in psychotherapy and which has become the basis for other theories, even those directly in con-flict with it. Freud's contribution to the theory of dreaming was very sig-nificant. Even though many of his concepts are questioned today, he brought dreams back to light in an era when they were ignored.

Even after Freud came forth with his theory of dreams, he noted an ap-parent lack of interest in the topic. Freud expressed his dissatisfaction with this state of affairs by accusing analysts of having nothing more to say about the dream, as though the whole subject were over and done with. Several years later, however, there appeared to be a renewed interest in the dream, and Fleiss summarized some of the literature on dreams, elaborating on several of Freud's concepts in his book *The Revival of Interest in the Dream* (1953). Fleiss reviews some of the writings on different types of dreams, such as telepathic, prophetic, and hypnotic dreams, as well as on applied dream interpretation, concluding:

> As for the analyst of today, no one could now maintain—as Freud did two decades ago—that he "acts as though he had nothing to say" to the dream; even a cursory glance at the table of contents of the present volume shows a wealth of subordinate subjects and proves that interest in the dream has been revived. (Fleiss, 1953, p. 127)

Later analysts have questioned many of Freud's concepts, particularly the wish-fulfillment nature of dreams and the sexual nature of symbols. Carl Jung was one of those analysts who made a break with Freud. Jung had read Freud's works and developed a regular correspondence with him, later paying him a visit. They had mutual admiration for each other, and Freud decided that Jung was to be his successor. However, a break in their relationship developed, and Jung questioned many of Freud's ideas. Whereas Freud viewed the dream as a disturbed mental activity through which he could explore his patients' neurosis, Jung saw the dream as a normal, creative expression of the unconscious. According to him, the function of the dream was "to restore our psychological balance by producing dream material that re-establishes, in a subtle way, the total psychic equilibrium" (Jung, 1964, p. 34). Jung viewed the dream as having a compensatory function, presenting some inner truth not yet known or not yet adequately trusted by consciousness. Jung rejected Freud's disguise theory completely, instead concentrating on the manifest content of the dream to find out what it might reveal rather than what it may be concealing. He also did not feel that all dreams were forms of infantile sexual wish-fulfillment needs; instead, he emphasized the present situation in the life of the dreamer rather than some past infantile fantasy. Most of all, Jung objected to Freud's reduction of all symbols to a single idea, feeling that such a system denied the uniqueness of particular symbols. Jung replaced this method with one that derived universal symbols from mythological parallels as well as the dreamer's own associations to the symbols. He stated, "No dream symbol can be separated from the individual who dreams it, and there is no definite or straightforward interpretation of any dream" (Jung, 1964, p. 38). He also reported many symbols that are collective instead of individual in origin, which he viewed as archetypes of the collective unconscious.

Jung believed that "a dream can contain some message other than the sexual allegory" (Jung, 1964, p. 13) and that these messages from the unconscious were more important than most people realize. To arrive at these messages, Jung believed that the dream should be interpreted in the way that the dreamer found most useful. Jung disagreed with Freud's method of free association, which he felt led away from the text of a dream. Instead, he wanted to keep as close as possible to the structure of the dream itself. He added other methods to interpretation to arrive at a dream's meaning. Sometimes he had the dreamer concentrate his or her attention on a particular dream image and notice what happened to that image. As the image underwent a series of changes, it could bring to light unconscious material. He also encouraged patients to represent significant dreams and images in the form of artistic expression. At other times, he let the dreamer "be" the various people and objects in the dream. Jung also differed from Freud by utilizing a series of dreams derived from a patient rather than focusing on a single dream.

There were three major steps in the Jungian approach to interpreting dreams, according to James Hall (1983). These include: (a) a clear understanding of the exact details of the dream; (b) a gathering of associations and amplifications in progressive order on a personal, cultural, and archetypal level; and (c) the placing of the amplified dream in the context of the dreamer's life. Jung was not very specific about his methodology of dream interpretation. Greene (1979) quotes Jung as saying that he had no theory of dreams and was not even sure that his way of handling dreams deserved to be termed a *method*. Jung felt that if one meditates on a dream long enough, some meaning will eventually reveal itself. In spite of his lack of a specific method for understanding dreams, Jung made important contributions in his deviations from Freud. Perhaps most significant was opening up the possibility that dream interpretation could be employed by psychotherapists who did not have a strictly psychoanalytic orientation or use only psychoanalytic methods.

Other psychoanalysts have also made certain changes in Freud's method and theory of dream interpretation. Whereas Freud saw the fulfillment of sexual wishes as the central role of dreams, French and Fromm (1964) emphasized the problem-solving functions of dreams. In addition, they attempted to provide more scientific basis and criticalness to interpretation. Whereas Freud's method of interpretation was primarily intuitive, in that the analyst's unconscious understood the patient's unconscious, French and Fromm's system was based on logical reasoning. In the first stage of their system of interpretation, the analyst uses intuition to form hypotheses; in the second stage, the analyst checks the evidence for these hypotheses. French and Fromm believed that the analyst should not force the evidence into a preconceived notion, but should apply systematic critical evaluation of interpretations, letting the data speak for itself. According to them: "An objectively critical approach to interpretation is an art that must be learned" (French & Fromm, 1964, p. 26). French and

Fromm illustrate their approach with several detailed analyses of dreams; however, their theory and method are primarily psychoanalytic, and the hypotheses are psychoanalytically based. Although they go into some detail in outlining their method, it is not one that can easily be understood or utilized by the average, nonpsychoanalytic clinician.

Richard Jones summarizes contributions of analysts in addition to Jung and French and Fromm to the theory of dreaming in his book *The New Psychology of Dreaming* (1970). He examines the interpretive approaches of Alfred Adler and Erik Erikson, among others. According to Adler, dreams express the unity of personality and are problem-solving, forward-looking experiences that produce emotions that can carry over to waking life. Adler viewed dreams as purposeful, focusing not only on unconscious conflicts, but on the dreamer's motivations, aspirations, and concerns for the future. For Adler dreams are a reflection of the personality and life-style of the dreamer and serve as rehearsals for future situations, where one can practice the next day's activity in a dream the preceding night. Adler, like Jung, disagreed with the use of universal symbols in dreams. He asserted that the content of the dream is a reflection of the private logic of the dreamer, and every dreamer has his or her own unique language. Adler viewed dream interpretation as an art requiring skill, sensitivity, and imagination, which needed to be kept within the logic and language of the client. He refused to set rules for interpreting dreams, in line with his view that interpretation was mainly an art (Gold, 1979).

Like Adler, Erikson viewed the dream as reflective of the dreamer's life-style, and he provided an outline for its systemic analysis to be used in research. The analysis, however, has never been used in research. Jones also summarizes the psychological functions of dreaming which he sees as analogous to biological functions. These include a neutralizing function, a reorganizing function, an alerting function, and a stimulating function. Jones emphasized the adaptive value of dreams.

More recent psychoanalysts have also elaborated on or taken issue with Freud's basic theory of dreams. Fosshage (1983), for example, proposes theoretical revisions to psychoanalytic dream interpretation. He states that in classical psychoanalysis, dreams have been recognized as indicators of latent wishes but that they have not been sufficiently recognized for their other functions. He feels that not enough emphasis has been given to the primarily developmental, regulatory, conflict-resolving, and reorganizational functions of dreams.

Another Freudian-trained psychoanalyst who took issue with Freud on the subject of dreams was Fritz Perls, the founder of Gestalt therapy. Perls rejected the idea of an unconscious and focused instead on the here and now. He saw the dream as an existential message, contrasting this to Freud's view of the dream as wishful thinking. Perls noted that the difference between Gestalt therapy and other types of therapy was ". . . essentially that we do *not* analyze. We *integrate*" (Perls, 1969, p. 66). He termed dreams the "royal road to integration," as opposed to Freud's view of them as the royal road to the unconscious. Perls believed that all the different parts of the dream are fragments of our personalities and that these fragments need to be put together to become a whole. He stated that people need to re-own these protected, fragmented parts of their personalities, and he did this by having them experience the dream and acting it out. In doing so, each dreamer would *become* the different aspects of the dream until the dreamer owned them and integrated them into his or her personality. Perls' technique essentially involved individual therapy in a group setting and made use of role-play and other experiential techniques to help the dreamer integrate disowned parts. He described his method as follows: " . . . my whole technique develops more and more into *never, never interpret*" (Perls, 1969, p. 121).

Perls introduced the concepts of topdog and underdog, which other dream analysts have incorporated into their approaches. The topdog is the self-righteous and authoritarian part of the personality that makes unrealistic, perfectionistic demands of the underdog, the part of the personality that manipulates by whining, wheedling, or acting like a child. The conflict between underdog and topdog is never resolved, and Perls attempted to have people integrate those two aspects of themselves.

Recent psychotherapists who have worked with dreams appear to have been heavily influenced by Perls' ideas, although their methods of interpretation may be different. Ann Faraday (1972; 1974) is another psychoanalytically trained analyst who takes issue with Freud. She utilizes many of Perls' and Jung's concepts, emphasizing the present rather than the past-oriented nature of dreams. She rejects the wish-fulfillment and disguise components of Freudian theory and believes that dreams can be interpreted objectively. For example, if a person dreams that his or her car brakes don't work, there may be something wrong with the car. She notes that the first step in dream interpretation is to check for possible truth about the external world, particularly when the dream refers to real people or situations. Only after exploring a dream thoroughly for signs of objective truth should one take it as a mirror reflecting subjective attitudes toward life. Many dreams can be interpreted on more than one level. Faraday uses Gestalt techniques to arrive at the dream message. She summarizes her method as one of allowing various dream images to speak for themselves until a topdog and an underdog emerge and the nature of the conflict becomes clear. The nature of the underdog gives a clue about a particular gap in the personality that must be reclaimed by making the underdog stand up to the topdog and assert itself. She suggests then retrieving that hole in the personality. Rather than speak of the unconscious, Faraday prefers to speak of "alienation," which refers to aspects of self that are disowned.

Gayle Delaney is another psychotherapist who has written on dreams and appears to have been influenced by Gestalt theory. Although she uses Gestalt concepts, what is most significant about her work is the clarity of her method. Delaney uses show business language to describe the function of dreams. She states that we are the producers of our own dreams, the writers of our own screenplays, the directors of our dream shows, and the stars of our dream scenes. Delaney offers practical guidelines for a dreamer to incubate a dream and interpret its meaning. In her dream interviewing method, she asks the dreamer to define and describe his or her symbols to her as though she were someone from another planet. She also describes how to move from the definition of an object to its underlying meaning. Delaney is probably one of the first dream analysts to offer detailed, concise guidelines on how to approach dream interpretation. Her book *Living Your Dreams* (1979) is geared primarily for the layman rather than the therapist.

Ernest Rossi is another current therapist who has made a contribution to the study of dreams. Rossi has been influenced by Jung and Milton Erikson, the hypnotherapist. In his book *Dreams and the Growth of Personality* (1972), he views dreams as creative processes leading to new levels of awareness in psychotherapy. In his "growth" psychotherapy, he elaborates on the concept of psychosynthesis "as the integration of two or more states of being or awareness to create a new aspect of identity" (Rossi, 1972, p. 161). This usually takes the form of dialogue between one's conscious attitudes and the autonomous forces of imagination. What emerges is gradually synthesized into identity and actualized as behavior.

All of the previously discussed theories have several features in common. All have the underlying assumption that dreams reveal aspects of personality. Furthermore, they implicitly assume that these parts of personality are either repressed, disowned, alienated, or not part of conscious awareness. Similarly, all attempt to bring integration or synthesis of these parts to consciousness. The theories differ as to the nature of the material disowned, whether it is repressed, neurotic, unacceptable material or whether it reflects healthy aspects of the personality. The theorists place varying emphasis on pathology versus growth in their theories of dreams. In addition, there is disagreement among the different theories on the extent of discrepancy between the manifest and latent dream content. There appears to be a continuum between objective and subjective interpretations, with some theorists believing that many dreams can be interpreted on a number of levels. Most of the theories differ from the classic Freudian view that dreams are merely wish fulfillments of infantile sexual wishes and instead stress that the dream serves other functions. Most believe that dreams contain important messages for the dreamer. Similarly, most theories are directly opposed to the Freudian reduction of all dream symbols to sexual ones, and most have the implicit assumption that symbols are individual to the dreamer.

Whereas most dream theories have several features in common, they differ as to the method of interpretation. The means of interpreting dreams range from Freud's free association to Perls' experiential methods. Many of the theorists discuss interpretation as an intuitive process, with few guidelines for the interested practitioner. Gayle Delaney is the only one who goes into specific detail in describing her method. However, she only discusses how to arrive at the meanings of symbols without elaborating on other steps in dream interpretation.

Hattie Rosenthal's (1980) contribution to dream interpretation is not so much in providing a theoretical framework, as in outlining a step-by-step, detailed method of interpretation. Her method of interpretation is comprehensive, detailed, specific, and teachable. Significant for its clarity and attention to detail, it is illustrated in later chapters at some length.

NONPSYCHOLOGICAL THEORIES
OF DREAMING

In contrast to the theories which state that dreams have psychological meaning, there are a number of theories that view dreaming purely as a physiological activity without any psychological significance. A few of these theories will be reviewed briefly only because their authors have used them to refute psychological theories of dreaming.

Hobson and McCarley proposed a view of dreaming based on recent research in the neurobiology of dreaming (Hobson & McCarley, 1977; McCarley & Hobson, 1977). Their activation-synthesis hypothesis offers a non-Freudian view of dreaming and states, in essence, that physiological processes rather than psychological processes are the primary determinants of dreams and their formal characteristics. Specifically, their hypothesis states that dreaming occurs only during a complex CNS physiological state known as the desynchronized (D) state or D sleep and is instigated by a pontine physiological process. In addition, the dream's formal characteristics of distortion, incoherence, and bizarreness are also caused by a physiological process, the random discharge of neuronal units (FTG cells). Since Freud proposed that dreams and their formal characteristics were instigated by psychological processes, they conclude that his theory must be wrong.

Several authors have critiqued the activation-synthesis hypothesis, both on empirical and theoretical grounds. Vogel (1978) cites the following research evidence that does not support the hypothesis. First, dreaming is not limited to the D state and occurs in the absence of pontine processes. Second, forebrain activity, which can have mental correlates, is involved in the instigation and maintenance of most D sleep episodes, contrary to the activation-synthesis hypothesis, which states that pontine FTG cells are the sole generators of the D state. Third, the correlational evidence is in contradiction to the claim that the formal characteristics of dreams are related to pontine activation. It is on methodological grounds that Vogel critiques the activation-synthesis hypothesis: "Purely neurophysiological data—such as that used in the activation-synthesis hypothesis—cannot refute a purely psychological theory such as Freud's" (Vogel, 1978, p. 1534). Vogel elaborates further:

> Put in general terms, neurophysiological variables cannot be used to test a psychological theory of dreams (such as Freud's) when the correlation between the relevant psychological variables and the relevant physiological variables is unknown. Furthermore, even when the relevant psychophysiological correlations are known, the use of physiological variables to test a psychological theory provides only an indirect test of the theory. A direct test would involve only the psychological variables. In the case of Freud's dream theory, a direct psychological test has yet to be made. (Vogel, 1978, p. 1534)

Labruzza (1978) also critiques the activation-synthesis hypothesis from the point of view of theory construction and logical reasoning. He notes that Hobson and McCarley do not distinguish between the dream state, a neurophysiological process, and dreaming as a mental, subjective experience. He states:

> It is not valid to move freely between independent logical systems of description and explanation. One cannot add apples and oranges without appealing to a superordinate concept such as fruit. Likewise, wishes cannot trigger cells, and cells firing in the pons cannot determine the meaning and motive of dreams. (Labruzza, 1978, p. 1537)

He adds further that there is not currently any way to translate statements about cells and dream motives into a common superordinate language. He concludes that since modern science has not yet established a well-defined mind-body isomorphism, conclusions about the psychological meanings of dreams cannot be drawn from neurobiological data.

Others have attempted to integrate psychological theories of dreaming with neurobiological findings. Fiss (1983) states that while the neuropsychological substratum of dreaming cannot be dismissed, dreams and dream content characteristics can be psychologically determined. He attempts to bridge the gap between what is scientifically respectable and clinically relevant in terms of an experimental psychology of dreaming. After reviewing experimental findings, he concludes that a biological basis of dreaming is not sufficient for understanding dreams. He states that "if we want to understand dreaming, we had better learn something about dreamers. Brains don't dream; dreamers dream'' (Fiss, 1983, p. 150). He concludes: ''To understand dreams, we need *psychological* theories and concepts, and *psychological* methods and data to test them. If it is to be clinically relevant, dream research must become a discipline that is scientific as well as humanistic'' (Fiss, 1983, p. 158).

Nonpsychological theories of dreaming have taken other forms than the activation-synthesis hypothesis. Crick and Mitchison (1983) state that during REM sleep, the brain eliminates mental activity that might interfere with rational thought and activity. During the day, a brain makes more connections between brain cells than are needed for efficient memory and thinking, and the dream's function is to clear the brain of these unneeded, meaningless connections. Crick and Mitchison's view has implications beyond their discounting the psychological meaning of dreams. Their theory also suggests that it might be damaging to recall one's dreams because doing so might strengthen neural connections that should be gotten rid of.

Christopher Evans (1983) offers a different view, but one with implications similar to those of Crick and Mitchison. According to Evans' computer theory, ''dreaming might be our biological equivalent to the computer's process of program inspection'' (Evans, 1983, p. 171). Dreams allow an opportunity to integrate the day's experiences with memories stored in the brain. The information-processing function of dreams is stressed in this view, with the implication that one need not disturb this process by recalling dreams. Unlike Crick and Mitchison, however, Evans assigns importance to dreams, valuing them primarily for their problem-solving and creative functions. He cites examples of scientific discoveries and literary creations from dreams; for example, Samuel Taylor Coleridge's poem ''Kubla Khan'' and Robert Louis Stevenson's creation of Jekyll and Hyde through dream images. Although Evans' computer theory does not see dreams as reflections of unconscious conflicts, he still finds some common ground with the psychological theories.

> My computer theory, in which the brain is continually updating its vast library of programs during the off-line sleep phase, has one crucial element in common with the approaches of Jung and Freud, namely that dreams are not just gratuitous, purposeless, meaningless exercises performed by a brain with so much spare capacity that it chooses to wallow in episodic acts of self-indulgence, unconnected to its duties and behavior when the organism it directs is awake. (Evans, 1983, p. 217)

Others have attempted to integrate neurophysiological and psychological theories of dreaming. Dr. Morton Reiser, chairman of the psychiatry department at Yale and author of *Mind, Brain, Body: Toward a Convergence of Psychoanalysis and Neurobiology* (1984), is able to reconcile his psychoanalytic view of dreams with recent neurobiological findings. He states that Freud himself had not given up hope that brain science would ultimately provide relevant information. In Reiser's opinion, the psychoanalytic process provides a powerful tool for the study of human memory function because of its power to uncover memory traces. He illustrates this at length in the case of Carol, a patient who was able to retrieve long-term childhood repressed memories through dreams and use these to help her in her present conflicts. Reiser proposes that the pattern of memory "storage" that Freud described as underlying the relationships of manifest dream contents to latent dream thoughts can be detected in the individual dream and in the patterning of stored memories that underly later repetitive and enduring patterns of adult behavior. Traces of such events left encoded in memory can be thought of as *nodal* points, which Reiser feels could have a neurobiological basis. He proposes that hypotheses from the "raw data" from the clinical psychoanalytic process can be empirically tested in the laboratory in an attempt to correlate them with neurophysiological events.

Similar to Jones' (1968) differentiation between theories of dreams and theories of dreaming, current theorists are attempting to reconcile research on dream formation and dream activity with theories on the psychological meanings of dreams. It must be remembered that Freud postulated his theory of dreams and dreaming in the absence of any of the recent scientific evidence for dreams and that his theories of dream formation and the functions of sleep were almost an afterthought and were irrelevant to his theory of dreaming.

Ironically, there is some physical evidence for several Freudian theories, particularly the role of dreams and the origin of the unconscious, which has been provided by a neuroscientist, Jonathon Winson, and described in his book *Brain and Psyche: The Biology of the Unconscious* (1985). Winson proposes a neuroscientific theory to explain Freud's observations and cites evidence for the unconscious, which represents the functioning of brain systems that are fixed early in childhood. He states his hypothesis:

> I believe that the phylogentically ancient mechanisms involving REM sleep, in which memories, associations and strategies are formed and handled by the brain as a distinct category of information in the prefrontal cortex and associated structures, are in fact the Freudian unconscious. (Winson, 1985, p. 209)

Winson supplies evidence for his view that dreaming provides a time for processing the day's events, a time when people file away new information with related memories. According to him, dreams serve to fix experiences in the mind and "dreaming is the bridge between brain and psyche" (Winson, 1985, p. 6). He states: "In man, dreams are a window on the neural process whereby, from early childhood on, strategies for behavior are being set down, modified or consulted'' (Winson, 1985, p. 209).

Attempts to integrate psychological and neuroscientific theories of dreaming are still in the early stages. As yet, there is no comprehensive theory of dreaming that takes into account both biological and psychological aspects of behavior. Dream theory and research are also in the very early phases, and it will probably take several decades before a reconciliation of the objective and subjective theories will occur.

CURRENT APPLICATIONS OF DREAMS IN PSYCHOTHERAPY

So far we have described different views of dreaming and different methods of dream interpretation to help the patient in psychotherapy achieve self-awareness. Dreams have also been used as adjuncts with other forms of therapy. The combination of hypnotherapy and dream analysis has been effective in psychotherapy. Rossi has combined hypnosis with dream analysis to synthesize different aspects of personality. In his tape *Hypnotic Dreams**, Rossi demonstrates the use of hypnosis with two individuals, Laura and Stanley, in helping them work through their dreams while in a hypnotic state.

Others have combined dreams and hypnosis as well. Scott (1982) states that for the patient in hypnoanalysis, dream interpretation can be helpful as another means of shortening the therapeutic process, since the dream frankly expresses the patient's conflict. After the therapist gives the patient the suggestion to dream about the root of his or her problem, principles of rapid dream interpretation are utilized in therapy. Scott provides examples of how this is done and what the therapist should watch for in dreams.

Dreams have also been utilized in other ways in psychotherapy. Doweiko (1982) has shown how rational emotive therapy can be used in working with dreams. He believes that the dreamer's contact with reality, although decreased, is still existent in the dream state. The dreamer works on his or her problems during the dream in an altered state of consciousness in which the demands of reality are not as pressing. Doweiko demonstrates how the themes of humiliation and rejection in the dreams of depressed patients reinforce the depression. The patient can learn to bring the dream experience under the focus of a cognitively oriented process and challenge his or her depressive cognitions.

*Rossi, E. *Hypnotic Dreams*, presented at the 1983 International Congress on Ericksonian approaches to Hypnosis and Psychotherapy, in Phoenix, Arizona. Available at the Milton H. Erickson Foundation, Inc., 3606 North 24th Street, Phoenix, Arizona, 85016.

Himelstein (1984) has also used the dream content in a novel way in psychotherapy. He discusses the relationship of the symbolic content of dreams to psychoanalytic and Gestalt theories of dream analysis. He asserts that the value of the dream in psychotherapy may not necessarily be the material that is uncovered, but that the dream content may serve as a stimulus for the production of clinically important material that may be of value in a particular therapeutic situation.

Like Himelstein, Werman (1978) relates uses of dreams other than the development of self-awareness in patients. He distinguishes between psychoanalysis and psychotherapy in terms of the dimensions of depth of exploration, frequency of visits, and duration of treatment. Psychoanalysis is insight-oriented therapy, with dreams functioning to bring awareness of conflicts. Psychotherapy is seen as having a supportive function, and dreams, if used at all, also serve supportive functions. Werman states that dreams provide material on three areas: unresolved childhood conflicts, the current life situation, and the therapeutic situation. The therapist's interpretation to the patient can include any or all three of these areas. What the therapist communicates to the patient about the dream should be related to the context of the particular patient's psychological life at the time. The therapist needs to assess the patient's emotional state before offering an interpretation. It would be unproductive to make interpretations unrelated to conscious concerns, since this may elicit rage, anxiety, or guilt on the part of the patient. Unlike interpretations in psychoanalysis that attempt to produce insight by uncovering repressed material, interpretations in supportive psychotherapy attempt to fortify ego defenses or strengthen the therapist-patient relationship.

Miller, Stinson, and Soper (1982) also discuss the use of dreams in nonanalytic psychotherapy. They stress the importance of dream discussions within a counseling framework and the implications for counselors using dreams. They state that dreams can be used as an additional avenue for setting up and maintaining therapeutic contact with clients. They view dreams as another mode of interaction in therapy, similar to art, music, writing, quotations, photographs and portraits, stating: "It is recommended here that counselors consider seriously another mode of interaction: dream discussions" (Miller, Stinson & Soper, 1982, p. 144). They suggest specific dream questions and techniques for the counselor who would like to make maximum use of dreams in counseling. The twelve dream questions they suggest include, "What in the dream does not fit with your everyday experience?"; "How did the dream end?"; and "What does this dream tell me about you?" The questions are primarily focused on the client's interpretation of the dream and his or her reactions and feelings about it. Unlike psychoanalytic interpretations, the questions focus on the present, and the counselor is not cast into the role of the all-knowing expert.

Merrill and Cary (1975) also discuss the use of dreams to focus on present conflicts. They explored the effectiveness of dream analysis in brief psychotherapy with college students. Dreams helped elucidate reality problems for students who were generally resistant to self-exploration. Dream interpretations in this case were based on readily assimilated and currently meaningful experience. Interpretation of the current significant conflicts increased participation in psychotherapy and helped students participate actively in therapy.

Dream analysis has also been used in sex therapy. Levay and Weissberg (1979) state that dreams can provide an understanding of unconscious factors that can cause and maintain sexual dysfunction and interfere with treatment. They note that by combining sex therapy with dream analysis, treatment is more likely to be successful and completed in less time than by either sex therapy or dream analysis alone. They use several examples to illustrate the interpretive use of dreams in sex therapy.

Dream analysis has also been used in group settings. Ullman and Zimmerman describe how to work with dreams in groups in their book *Working with Dreams* (1979). In their work, participants relate their dreams in a group setting, and other group members project to the dream as though it were their own. This helps the dreamer integrate his or her dream experience with the help of others. Ullman and Zimmerman differentiate between their dream-appreciation groups and group psychotherapy. Whereas the emphasis in group psychotherapy is on the interpersonal relationships between group members, in the dream-appreciation groups, the focus is on the relation of the dreamer to the dream. Ullman and Zimmerman describe their process of working with dreams as having four distinct stages, three within the group and a fourth one later when the group finishes the dream work. In the first stage, the dreamer relates a dream to the group. In the second stage, group members make the dream their own, stating what feelings it evokes in them and associating to the symbols. The dreamer is fully in control of the dream at all times, in that he or she merely listens and is free to accept or reject what is said. In the third stage, the dream is given back to the dreamer, who shares his or her reactions. Then the group asks the dreamer questions to help him or her reconstruct the life context leading to the dream. After the group work is over, the dreamer is encouraged to look at the dream alone. This constitutes the fourth stage. Ullman and Zimmerman stress the importance of having the dreamer feel safe in a group environment and completely in control of how much to reveal.

Several authors have demonstrated the use of dreams in family and marital therapy. Perlmutter and Babineau (1983) describe the utilization of dreams within the context of couples' therapy. Their approach stresses the interpersonal aspects of couples sharing dreams with each other.

When a spouse shares a dream in conjoint therapy, it becomes a significant moment in which unconscious communication between the couple becomes manifest. Perlmutter and Babineau suggest that therapy can be more effective when the interpersonal dimensions of a dream, rather than its intrapsychic ones, are highlighted. Cirincione, Hart, Karle, and Switzer (1980) also describe the use of dreams in marital and family therapy. Rather than focusing on the content of dreams, they present a process-based method for using dreams as an adjunct to conjoint therapy. Dreams are viewed as pictures of feelings and as guides to the dynamics operating within each family member.

Bynum (1980) also emphasizes a process rather than a content orientation in using dreams in family therapy. In this approach, family members share and actively participate in the shared dreams of each other at various levels. Bynum asserts that the dreams of families in and out of therapy reflect the major emotional issues of that family. He has family members keep a dream log and share their dreams with each other, believing that dreams clearly reflect family alliances and bring out shared family myths. The process of sharing these dreams with other family members generally leads to more differentiation within the family. Bynum suggests several techniques in working with dreams, including contrasting and comparing dreams of different family members or having each person say what the dream means for him. Bynum states in conclusion: "The dream is the primary process mode and closer to the heartbeat of the family" (Bynum, 1980, p. 230).

Dreams have also been used to diagnose and treat psychosomatic illness. Bressler and Mizrachi (1978a; 1978b) describe how a single dream can be a useful diagnostic tool for the primary physician in working with psychosomatic patients. They discuss the use of dream interpretation by physicians working with asthmatic patients. They provide examples of how dreams, accompanied by the patient's history, including all psychosomatic illnesses, may be useful both in diagnosis and in brief supportive psychotherapy. This makes the use of dreams valuable not only for the psychotherapist, but for other practitioners who are dealing with the underlying emotional aspects of disease. The relationship of dreams to the formation of psychosomatic illness has also been discussed by Warnes (1982), who uses clinical vignettes to demonstrate and illustrate that relationship. That dreams can correlate with and reflect bodily states has been amplified by Arnold Mindell in his book *Dreambody* (1982). He demonstrates how dream interpretation can enrich and clarify the meaning of physical symptoms. In dreambody work, dreams appear as pictures of bodily processes that are occurring at the present. The dreamer experiences how dreams are intimately connected to body problems. Mindell demonstrates the use of bodywork to solve these problems.

Other innovative uses of dreams have been utilized in working with children. Elyse Jacobs (1982) describes the Dream Theatre as an art form working from children's dreams. Small groups of children, ages 5 to 12, meeting once or twice weekly for eight sessions, first draw their dream allies, dream beings who have proved helpful. Then they share their dreams and create puppets of their allies. The children then work with a theme, thinking about it before sleeping as well as visualizing their ally. They try to capture these images while dreaming, and later bring these to the classroom where they use both their puppets and other children to act out the dream. The children are also instructed to change their dreams in class and later in their sleep. The creation of an ally helps the child develop that helpful part of his or her own psyche and deal with night fears.

In her book *Your Child's Dreams* (1984), Patricia Garfield also discusses the use of dreams with children to help them cope more adaptively. She feels that the themes of childhood dreams develop into those of adult dreams and that we can direct children to take more control of their dreams. In her study of 288 dreams of 120 children, she found that the majority of children's dreams had "bad dream" themes. She worked out seven principles to move children into "happy dreaming," methods that help the child deal with the hostile figures in his or her dream. She teaches children the process of "redreaming"—fantasizing a different ending to a dream—as a method to help them learn different ways of coping. She also teaches them to use dream allies to their advantage.

Jokipaltio (1982) also discusses working with children's dreams. She states that while children may have wish-fulfillment dreams, many of their dreams are more complicated. She contends that children have more anxiety dreams than adults and that they tell these dreams more often than they do pleasant ones. She also thinks that a child's dream involves the same distortions as an adult's. Jokipaltio describes how dreams of children help illuminate aspects of psychotherapy. She illustrates the case of a 5-year-old girl whose dreams involved elements of transference.

The use of dreams to elucidate transference and countertransference reactions in therapy has also been emphasized as one of the uses of dreams for the therapist and client. Martin (1982) discusses the implications of dreams in which the analyst appears undisguised. He describes the ways in which the fears and needs of patients express themselves in dreams and how the analyst can understand and interpret the dreams. J. A. Hall (1984) also provides examples of how the dreams of therapists and patients can be helpful in stabilizing the transference/countertransference situation. Similarly, Spero (1984) illustrates the use of dreams in helping the analyst deal with his or her own feelings toward patients. He discusses his own countertransference dream, which helped clarify feelings that may have remained hidden and which aided in dealing with conflicts.

Similar to their role in elucidating transference and countertransference reactions, dreams have also been used to help supervisees clarify their feelings about their supervisors. Langs (1982) discusses the hypothesis that dreams reported to supervisors by their psychoanalytic student supervisees contain the supervisee's unconscious perceptions and projections about the supervisor and the therapeutic techniques. Langs presents a model of supervision that uses latent and manifest dream material, illustrated by dreams reported by supervisees. Langs makes it clear that he does not imply that supervisors should request from their supervisees the reports of dreams. However, when these dreams are spontaneously reported, it is generally at a time of supervisory crisis. Langs suggests that supervisees report their dreams to their supervisors ''as a means of conveying highly significant perceptions and fantasies that are either entirely repressed within the supervisee, or too dangerous to communicate directly in supervision'' (Langs, 1982, p. 594). According to Langs, the supervisor should make an effort to understand what the dream is stating about the relationship, searching the dream not only for the supervisee's difficulties, but also for possible countertransference and mistakes on his or her part. In this way, the dream may be an adaptive way to deal with a treatment or supervisory crisis.

CONCLUSION

The uses of dreams in clinical practice have been varied and not limited to any theoretical orientation. In addition to facilitating insight in psychotherapy, dreams have also been used in systems approaches where the content has not been as important as the process. Dreams have been used as adjuncts to other methods in therapy, and the combination of dreams with other tools has generally been considered effective.

Chapter 2
Research on the Use of Dreams in Psychotherapy

Although there are many theories regarding the functions of dreams, the experimental literature on dreams and their uses in psychotherapy have been very sparse. There appear to be several reasons for this. The investigation of psychotherapeutic effectiveness is a complex one, and outcome studies are fraught with difficulties (Goldstein & Dean, 1966). In addition to all of the problems associated with psychotherapy research, studies on dreams also present problems of their own. Webb and Cartwright (1978), in their review of the status of dream research, cite two general explanations for the paucity of dream studies. One is the attitude that dreams, being unobservable, cannot be studied by the methods that are proper to the study of psychology. Another reason for the limited research in the area is a practical one. The working conditions under which dreams are collected are difficult ones, as experimenters must gather their data at night while their subjects are sleeping. A great deal of effort is required in order to obtain results from even one subject. This has generally resulted in small N studies, with very few attempts at replication. In addition, the nature of dreams makes it difficult to carry out manipulative studies. The combination of problems associated with psychotherapy research and dream research has resulted in very few controlled studies on the effectiveness of dreams in psychotherapy. Most of the existing studies have been descriptions of cases, and few researchers have attempted to systematically assess the validity of dream theories or their clinical effectiveness under controlled conditions. This chapter will review some applications of dream research to dream analysis.

The impetus for dream research began with an important discovery by Aserinsky and Kleitman (1953) of rapid eye movements during sleep. Dement and Kleitman (1957a; 1957b) then conducted a number of experiments where subjects were awakened during various phases of sleep. They found that subjects awakened during rapid eye movements had a high incidence of dream recall. Having established a physiological basis of dreaming, the researchers have found that dreaming occurs at regular intervals, with an average of four or five dreams per night. Kleitman's and Dement's results have been confirmed by other studies, all of them showing that the REM (rapid eye movement) period is one in which subjects recall dreams. REM sleep has also been referred to as the D state for dreaming. Later studies have shown that dreaming also occurs in non-REM periods (Foulkes, 1962; Rechtschaffen, Verdone, & Wheaton, 1963). These mental phenomena are less vivid, visual, or intense and more concerned with current events. The demonstration of dreams in the laboratory has been important, particularly in dispelling the myth that not everyone dreams.

Whereas there has been much research on the physiology of dreaming, studies on the psychology of dreaming have been less frequent. The meaning of dreams is difficult to study, since only the manifest content of dreams is open to experimental investigation. Studies on psychological aspects of dreams have generally taken several forms. One line of investigation has been to study the extent to which dreams are a mirror of personality and waking experiences. In these studies, dreams and waking experiences are correlated to assess to what extent dream characteristics relect waking concerns. A second line of investigation is to specifically manipulate presleep conditions and study their effect on the dreams. A third research method has been to manipulate the dream and study its effects on subsequent waking behavior. Studies have also been conducted to assess certain hypotheses or aspects of psychological theories, and some researchers have developed specific methodologies for the measurement of dreams. Only a few studies are reported on the effectiveness of dreams in psychotherapy. Much of the literature on this topic is anecdotal, based on a few cases, with few controlled studies in this area. Some of the studies and findings on dreams and their psychological significance will be reviewed.

DREAMS AS REFLECTIONS
OF PERSONALITY

To what extent do dreams mirror the dreamer's waking personality and experiences? This is a difficult question to answer, since only the manifest content of a dream can be investigated experimentally. One of the pioneers who attempted to study this question scientifically was Calvin Hall (1947), who described his method of studying dreams. Hall stated that the dream has two characteristics that make it possible to be investigated scientifically. First, it is a personal document, and second, it is a projection. He wrote, "In our opinion, the dream is more purely personal and more purely projected than any other material which the psychologist has available for the study of personality" (Hall, 1947, p. 68). Hall felt that the major problem with psychoanalytic writings was that they did not meet the standards of the scientific method. Most of this work was anecdotal and failed to recognize the importance of control or statistical analysis of data. Hall thus set out to make a scientific study of dreams for the purpose of establishing the interpretation of dreams as a valid method for diagnosing personality. He collected and studied 10,000 dreams of normal people through what he termed the "dream series" method. Dream series were collected from college students in psychology classes. Following two surveys where students recorded their dreams either in the classroom or directly upon awakening, Hall devised a standardized form for recording dreams. After the dreams were collected, they were then coded in order to conceal the dreamer's identity. This was done both to help students report dreams of a highly personal nature and to prevent information about the dream that had been obtained from other sources from influencing the interpretation of the dream series. (The terms *series* and *cycle* refer to the dreams reported by an individual.) The third step was the analysis and interpretation of the dream series. This step was the most problematic, since a dream can be interpreted in different ways depending upon the interpreter's theory. Hall viewed dreams as projections of the person's inner dynamics, which represent attempts to resolve his or her current conflicts. Hall felt that a single dream could not be properly analyzed unless the interpreter had a great deal of knowledge about the dreamer. However, if it is necessary to know the person's dynamics before understanding the dream, of what value is dream interpretation? To overcome this dilemma, Hall substituted the analysis of a dream cycle for the analysis of a single dream. The dreams of a cycle are studied to look for major conflicts, and other dreams of the series are scrutinized for signs of the same conflict. Usually one dream, the spotlight dream, will highlight this conflict more than others. If a number of dreams of the same individual are consistent with the same interpretation, that interpretation is felt to be validated. If the interpretation of the spotlight dream is not supported by other dreams, then another hypothesis is formed and tested out in the same manner, by applying it to other dreams. The individual dreams are then fitted together by testing one hypothesis after another until a coherent and meaningful interpretation is obtained. Hall provides several illustrations of this method, which is used to attain a diagnosis of the dreamer's inner conflicts without any other data than the dream series. In other words, the meaning of the dream is found within the dream itself. How valid is this method of interpretation? Hall discusses the validation of dream analysis by the methods of social agreement, internal agreement, external agreement, agreement with the future, and agreement with the past and presents evidence for the validity of dream analysis obtained from the application of several of these methods.

In 1953, Hall published the results of his work in his book *The Meaning of Dreams*. After studying the dreams of thousands of people using the dream series method, Hall attempted to classify what people dream about. His first method of classification was fourfold, consisting of settings, characters, actions, and emotions. Briefly, he found that most dream settings are familiar and commonplace, such as a house, a street, or a car. People dream of recreational settings more than work settings. The scarcity of work settings led Hall to suggest that people display an aversion to work and a liking for play in their dreams. The people that are dreamed about are usually those with whom the dreamer is emotionally involved. People rarely dream about prominent figures but generally about people who are associated in some way with their personal conflicts. The actions in dreams are varied, with the largest class of actions performed by the dreamer involving movement, including all changes in location, whether by walking, riding, climbing, or falling. Passive activities such as talking or sitting are common in dreams as well, with women being more passive than males. The emotions experienced in dreams are also varied, with unpleasant emotions of fear, anger, and sadness being twice as frequent as pleasant ones of joy or happiness. Hall found that dreaming on the whole is not a pleasurable pastime.

From his findings, Hall concluded that the dream is not a mysterious phenomena but a picture of what the mind is thinking. The dream reveals in a clear, economical manner the dreamer's present conflicts rather than long-repressed sexual wishes. The analysis of dream content reveals that, as a whole, the dreamer is concerned with him- or herself, the people he or she is directly involved with, and inner conflicts. Hall did not feel that dreams were intended to disguise and rejected the reduction of all symbols to sexual ones. He believed that there are many symbols for the same referent, and an individual's idea of the symbol must be identical with his or her idea of the referent. Hall's findings supported the notion of the individuality of symbols.

From his findings, Hall concluded that dreams are not esoteric or mysterious but simply projected pictures of people's thoughts, writing:

> Anyone who can look at a picture and say what it means ought to be able to look at his dream pictures and say what they mean. The meaning of a dream will not be found in some theory about dreams; it is right there in the dream itself. (Hall, 1953, p. 85)

In later years, Hall refined his method of analyzing dream content, describing it in his book *The Content Analysis of Dreams* (Hall & Van de Castle, 1966). The main contribution of Hall and Van de Castle was a methodological one, in that they presented a comprehensive system of classifying and scoring dreams. The authors also provided normative material based upon 1,000 dreams, as well as examples of scoring a dream series.

Like Hall, Offenkranz and Rechtschaffen (1963) attempted to study the relationship between waking and dream states. They looked at nightly dream sequences of a patient in psychotherapy on 15 different nights, during which 50 dreams were recorded. They found that despite the high variability of manifest content, all of the dreams of a night were concerned with either the same conflict or with a limited number of different conflicts. They believed that their data supported the hypothesis of a parallel between the sequence of waking behavior and the activities in the dream sequence.

Following Hall, many researchers have attempted to investigate the relationship between dreams and waking life. There are many problems associated with using dreams as dependent variables. Firstly, only the surface or manifest content of dreams is open to experimental investigation; arriving at the meaning of a dream would require a thorough knowledge of the subject. Secondly, there are many variables involved when we speak of personality or the waking state. One is the subject's long-term traits, another is short-term states such as hunger or thirst, and a third is the social environment of the laboratory. All of these would need to be isolated to assess the extent to which they are reflected in dreams.

In spite of the problems associated with this type of research, most of the studies support the premise that dreams accurately reflect waking characteristics and concerns. One area of research has been in comparison of men's and women's dreams. As noted previously, Hall (1953) found that women's dreams reflected more passive activity than men's dreams, consistent with cultural differences at the time. In a later report, Hall and Domhoff (1963) noted that men dreamed more frequently of other men, whereas women dreamed more equally of the two sexes. They explained this finding by stating that men's problems center more around other males than they do around females and that men were continuing their conflicts in their waking life in the dream state. Another study of sex differences in dreams was conducted by Winget, Kramer, and Whitman (1972). They found that women's dreams have more people, more friendliness, more emotion, more indoor settings, and more home and family concerns than men's dreams. Men's dreams were reported to have more aggression and striving or achievement. Phyllis Koch-Sheras (1985) re-examines the differences between men's and women's dreams in view of the changing culture of women. She states that studies on sex differences are at least ten years old, and that we can expect women's dreams to change with their changing role in society. As women are working outside the house, many of the dream settings are now also outside the home. Similarly, women are showing more concern with occupational status in dreams. In addition, recent dreams show more aggression in females, again reflecting their changing role in society. These findings suggest that dreams focus on and reflect the emotional preoccupations of waking life.

Cultural differences in dreams have also been studied. LeVine (1966) studied three groups of Nigerian school boys and was able to predict the frequency of achievement imagery in each group based on knowledge of the power system of each sociocultural group. Roll, Hinton, and Glazer (1974) studied death themes and images in dreams of Anglo-Americans and Mexican-Americans. They accurately predicted the higher number of death themes in Mexican-American women who were traditional culture carriers. The sociocultural differences in dreams support the continuity of waking and dreaming characteristics.

Another area that has assessed the continuity between dreaming and waking concerns has been in the study of depressed individuals (Beck & Ward, 1961; Hauri, 1976; Kramer, Whitman, Baldridge, & Lansky, 1966; Kramer, Whitman, Baldridge, & Ornstein, 1968; Langs, 1966; Miller, 1969; Van de Castle & Holloway, 1971). These studies on the whole show that depressed individuals have dreams with themes of masochism, dependency, helplessness, and hopelessness, similar to their waking states. In addition, the dreams are bland and barren, again consistent with their emotional states. These characteristics generally prevailed in dreams, even when the individuals were not acutely ill, suggesting that some of these depressive traits may be long-standing in nature.

Studies with different clinical groups are consistent with those of depressed patients. Kramer, Whitman, Baldridge, and Ornstein (1970) studied the dreams of paranoid schizophrenics early and later in their illnesses and found that there was a similarity between their dreaming and waking states. They found that the early dreams contained strangers and had aggressive themes. Okuma, Sunami, Fukuma, Takeo, and Motoike (1970) compared the dreams of chronic hebephrenics with those of an age-matched control group. Their findings indicated that in comparison to the dreams of control subjects, the patients' dreams were less organized and contained more direct sex and negative emotions. In addition, the dream characters were less often friendly. These results support the continuity between waking and dream states. The waking state, in which hebephrenics are more primitive in their expression of feelings and impulses, is reflected in the dream state.

Another study that supports the view that dreams are expressive of an individual's present situation is that of Kramer, Hlasny, Jacobs, and Roth (1976). If dreams are meaningful and express an individual's unique situation, then those of one person should be differentiated from another's. The authors had three judges sort out dreams of five normal and five schizophrenic subjects to see if they could identify which dreams came from the same person. The judges were able to sort dreams for each person correctly above chance levels and were even able to sort dreams that came from the same night. The authors concluded that dreams reflect people both in their stable, long-standing traits and in their more temporary states.

The research on the relationship between waking and dream concerns suggests that there is a continuity between them, with dreams mirroring waking behaviors. In spite of the difficulties associated with studying dreams in the laboratory, much of the research in this area suggests that dreams do accurately reflect personality.

THE EFFECT OF WAKING
CONDITIONS ON DREAMS

To what extent are dreams influenced by waking conditions? In this line of investigation, a specific presleep condition is induced, and its effect on the dream is measured. One difficulty with this research paradigm is that the experimenter must have knowledge of the meaning of the stimulus to the subject and the subject's symbolic language in the dreams.

Foulkes and Rechtschaffen (1964) compared the effect on subsequent dreaming of exposure to a television western film and to a quieter romantic comedy. They found that this viewing made little difference on the texts of the dreams but did affect their level of excitement. They did find, however, that the dream content following the more violent western film tended to be more vivid, imaginative, and emotionally charged than the dream content following the quieter film.

Witkin and Lewis (1967) elaborated on the research procedure used by Foulkes and Rechtschaffen (1964) and described their method for studying the unique and personal way in which thoughts and feelings in the waking state are transformed in later dreams. The subject undergoes an arousing experience just before sleeping, and this event then serves as the reference point for studying transformations. By means of a special technique, the content of the subject's reverie between the presleep experience and the time of actual sleep is sometimes obtained. Witkin and Lewis described a variety of methods for studying dreams following presleep manipulation. At the end of every sleep session, a full inquiry is conducted into each dream, including the subject's associations and reactions to it. Furthermore, each subject is intensively studied before and during the experiment, and this knowledge is supplemented by a biographical interview. A thorough knowledge of the subject is needed to connect the way in which a particular subject symbolizes the presleep event in dreams and relates it to his or her experience of the total experimental situation and to significant events in everyday life. Witkin and Lewis give examples of their method, which combines clinical work with laboratory methods, and conclude,

> Thus it seems possible to obtain in the laboratory dreams and enough of their relevant clinical context to permit their study in the manner followed in clinical work. More important, our procedure makes it possible to put to experimental test a number of concepts about dream phenomena, some of them in the clinical method of dream interpretation. (Witkin & Lewis, 1967, p. 201)

Breger, Hunter, and Lane (1971) collected dreams following real-life emotional experiences, such as following a group therapy session or preceding surgery. They stated that it is necessary to know how each subject responds to the waking situation in order to see the types of defense mechanisms the subject employs. After the subject's waking defenses are known, the dreams were found to be consistent with his or her waking emotional state. Although some common elements occurred across subjects who were in the same situation (for example, the act of cutting and of cut-out objects for individuals undergoing surgery), each subject had a unique way of representing his or her stress. Breger, Hunter, and Lane's study supports the notion that the emotional experiences of waking life can influence dreams.

Another kind of experimental manipulation of dream content has been to suggest to subjects that they dream about specific topics. Belicki and Bowers (1982) examined the role of hypnotizability in dream change. They gave 42 undergraduates a hypnotic susceptibility test and found that hypnotic ability correlated significantly with the amount of dream change. Their results suggest that presleep instructions can influence dreams.

Another study that indicates that persons can control their dreaming through presleep instructions has been conducted by Doyle (1984). Sixty-three undergraduates were administered the dream behavior survey schedules for pleasure and displeasure the first and fifteenth week of the semester. After providing one week of baseline data, ten subjects participated in three 2-hour skill sessions, and data were collected for 14 weeks using a daily dream record. In the skill sessions, self-suggestion, cognitive restructuring, control expectations, and dream record-keeping were taught. In the placebo group, twelve subjects read about dreams and kept daily dream records. The remaining 41 subjects took the pre- and posttreatment survey only. The findings suggested that the skill sessions were effective. Dreaming and behaviors associated with dreaming were significantly more pleasurable 12 weeks after the dream interventions and maintenance of a daily dream record. In addition, a 6-month follow-up showed that the changes were still in effect.

These studies have implications for psychotherapy. That subjects can influence their dreams through instruction is important, as clients in therapy are frequently asked to incubate dreams on certain issues. The therapist can ask the client to confront and change certain issues in his or her dream and work them out. In addition, these studies also support the premise that dreams are influenced by waking conditions and are not simply random, meaningless activity.

THE EFFECT OF DREAMS ON WAKING BEHAVIOR

What effect do dreams have on waking behavior? One line of investigation has been to study the effect of dream absence on subsequent waking behavior. Dement (1960) studied the effects of dream deprivation on eight subjects by awakening them at the beginning of a rapid eye movement period and keeping them awake for several minutes before allowing them to go back to sleep. By awakening subjects at the onset of every REM period and continuing this procedure for several nights, it was possible to bring about a 70% reduction in total REM time. It was found that subjects began dreaming at progressively shorter intervals after going back to sleep and that more frequent awakenings were necessary as the experiment proceeded. The dream deprivation experiments were done to determine whether a person could function normally without any dreaming. The results showed that several psychological disturbances developed during and after these experiments. The following disturbances were noted: tension and anxiety, with a major anxiety attack in one subject; a brief period of depersonalization in one subject; memory disturbances; problems in motor coordination; difficulties in concentration; irritability and hostility; and a disturbance in time sense in one subject. Two subjects showed a heightened tendency to produce transient hallucinations in response to photic flicker stimulation. When the subjects were allowed to dream, the psychological disturbances disappeared. None of the above described changes were apparent for control subjects who were awakened during NREM periods. Dement concluded that a person needs a minimum amount of dreaming and that deficits resulting from dream deprivation tend to be made up later. He suggested that the incipient hallucinatory phenomena reflected an attempt to break through the dream cycle in spite of experimental efforts to suppress it and that one of the functions of dreaming may be to prevent daytime hallucinations. The dream deprivation experiments support the implications that dreaming has an adaptive psychological function and may even ward off psychotic-like behavior.

In a later study, Dement (1964) observed the development of psychotic-like behavior in several subjects who were REM deprived for 15 or 16 continuous nights by a combination of forced awakenings and Dexedrine administration on some nights. One of the subjects showed paranoid behavior and became very suspicious of others; another displayed behavior that was very unusual for him. These psychological disturbances were more pronounced than in the previous studies, where subjects were dream deprived for less than a week. Once again, the disturbances disappeared when the subjects were allowed to dream. As in the previous study, this suggests that dreaming has adaptive psychological functions.

That dreams have psychological value and may even prevent daytime hallucinations is indirectly supported by studies on REM deprivation with schizophrenics. What happens when actively hallucinating individuals are deprived of REM sleep? Zarcone, Gulevich, Pivik, and Dement (1968) found that patients who are actively hallucinating during waking do not make up for the loss of REM time. Gillin and Wyatt (1975) dream-deprived schizophrenic patients with control patients who had other diagnoses for two nights each. Unlike the control patients, schizophrenics needed fewer awakenings, showed no increase in awakenings from the first night to the second night and no REM rebound on their recovery nights of uninterrupted sleep. These studies indirectly lend support to the idea that dreams or night hallucinations may serve the function of preventing day hallucinations.

Other studies have supported the adaptive functions of dreaming. Greenberg, Pillard, and Pearlman (1972) found that when REM sleep is intact, subjects handle situations that were previously stressful with less upset than after a night of REM-deprived sleep. Similarly, Cartwright (1974a), who attempted to study the effects of dreaming on problem solving, reported that problems are handled more realistically the next morning when REM sleep remains intact. Lewin and Glaubman (1975) showed that subjects score higher on tests of creative thinking following REM-present sleep than after REM-absent sleep.

Two studies by Fiss also lend support for the adaptive value of dreams. Fiss, Klein, and Shollar (1974) interrupted every REM period after 10 minutes of REM sleep in two subjects for four out of thirty nights in the sleep laboratory. They found that dream reports collected during the REM interruption nights were as long as those obtained during the REM completion nights. The subjects apparently made up for lost dream time even when they were not deprived of REM time. The REM interruption procedure seemed to help bring into focus the subjects' major preoccupations. The authors conclude that people may dream in order to concentrate on what troubles them most, perhaps to work out some type of solution.

In another study, Fiss and Litchman (1976) used a "dream enhancement" procedure, a method intended to encourage subjects to concentrate all their waking attention on dreams, on two psychiatric inpatients for seven nights, alternating between REM dream enhancement and NREM dream enhancement. Results showed that REM dream enhancement was significantly more often associated with symptom relief and increased self-awareness than NREM dream enhancement. The findings suggest that REM dreams help maintain and improve emotional well-being.

Although most studies suggest that individuals need a certain amount of dreaming and that dreams have an adaptive psychological function, there is still a great deal of confusion about the effect of dream absence on subsequent behavior. Cartwright (1978) summarizes these findings in her book *A Primer on Sleep and Dreaming*, citing evidence of positive waking changes in depressed individuals following REM reduction.

> We must think about the kind of personality structure involved, the level of deprivation, and where the effects will be tested: on the immediate sleep, the following waking, or on the next uninterrupted sleep. The sleep and dreaming deficits may be compensated for together or separately, and the effects may be obstructive, destructive, neutral, or absent. All of these seem possible. (Cartwright, 1978, p. 93)

In summary, studies of the effects of dreams on waking behavior suggest that in general most individuals require a certain amount of dreaming and tend to make it up when they are deprived of it. Dream deprivation can result in moderate to serious psychological disturbances, which are usually corrected when the person is allowed to dream again. These studies, as well as those that show that actively hallucinating patients do not make up for the loss of REM time when deprived of it, suggest a relationship between day and night hallucinations and that one of the functions of dreaming may be to prevent waking disturbances. Other research also supports the adaptive function of dreams. However, the issue is still a complex one, and further research on the effects of dreaming on waking behavior needs to focus on the personality structure, the amount of deprivation, and the specific type of effects of dream deprivation.

EXPERIMENTAL STUDIES OF PSYCHOLOGICAL THEORIES

Most of the investigations on dreaming have been of an exploratory nature, with very little research focused on the testing of specific theories or hypotheses generated from theories of dreaming. As noted previously, dream theories have emphasized several functions of dreams, including wish fulfillment of forbidden impulses, catharsis, assimilation of anxiety, prevention of psychological disturbances, information processing, and integration of different aspects of personality. Most of these hypotheses have not been tested in the laboratory, and the few studies we have only indirectly lend support to some of these hypotheses.

Trosman (1963) attempted to integrate dream research with the psychoanalytic theory of dreams. He examined four basic concepts of Freudian dream theory under the light of experimental findings. Freud's concept of the dream as the guardian of sleep is inconsistent with physiological evidence that there is no dreaming during the deep sleep of much of the night and that dreams occur during light sleep and the waking up process. Freud's assumption of the sleep-preserving function of dreams is unnecessary to his theory of dreaming, however, and as noted previously, is almost an afterthought to the fundamental concepts of his theory. Freud's proposition that dreams are an expression of unconscious wishes is not incompatible with the evidence. "Nevertheless," writes Trosman, "the experimental findings tend to throw doubt on the notion that dreaming is instigated solely by the pressure resulting from an upsurge of drive energy seeking release" (Trosman, 1963, p. 34). Freud's view of dreaming as a form of regression toward the perceptual end of the psychic apparatus is again not inconsistent with experimental findings. The biggest disparity between the research findings and Freud's theoretical formulation occurs in the area of the duration of dreams. Freud assumed that dreams occurred instantaneously, but experimental findings suggest that dreaming occurs over the same period of time that the action of the dream would require. Again, it is important to separate Freud's theory of dreams from his theory of dreaming. Trosman reviews the dream deprivation experiments of Dement and others, which suggest the possibility

> that one may not only dream to sleep, but perhaps also sleep to dream. Dreaming may be highly adaptive or even necessary as a mode of discharge for tension, conflicts, and anxiety which arise in waking life, and, in this sense, the importance of dreaming may far exceed the role it plays in its relationship to sleep. (Trosman, 1963, p. 36)

Schonbar (1961) conducted a study to test Freud's view that when patients forget dreams, it is due to resistance. Forty-five graduate students in education were divided into high- and low-recall groups on the basis of frequency of recalled dreams. Contrary to assertions that dreams from the falling asleep period are less likely to be remembered than those just before waking because of the long intervening period of unconsciousness, it was found for both groups that dreams preceding a waking period are not better remembered than dreams followed by continued sleep. For the frequent recallers, it was also found that dreams are more often remembered as having had emotional components than as having been neutral and that the feelings are more often unpleasant than pleasant. This was not so for the low-recall group, who also had significantly more neutral dreams than the high-recall group. It appears that emotional rather than temporal factors play a part in dream recall. It was concluded that the findings of this study support some of the propositions of Freudian dream theory, namely, that forgetting is not accidental, but due to resistance.

Reitav (1985) reviews some of the problems of dream recall studies that test Freud's hypothesis of repression and criticizes them on both methodological and theoretical grounds. His major theoretical concern about these studies has been that they have focused exclusively on repression as a psychological defense and have not looked at the broader spectrum of other defenses. Methodological problems have included using self-report diaries to assess recall and not having objective measures of defenses. Reitav corrected some of these methodological problems in a study of undergraduates. His results provide clear support that psychological defenses account for dream recall, although repression is not the only psychological defense. In addition, different conditions elicit different defenses.

The major concept in Freudian theory, the hypothesis that the function of the dream is to gratify forbidden impulses, has not been tested experimentally. Webb and Cartwright (1978) cite the multiple problems associated with the testing of this hypothesis:

> First, the level of a forbidden impulse must be increased and its presence validated without calling it to the attention of the subject. The expression of that impulse must be independently validated as present in the dreams in a way that discharges the tension associated with its build-up. With all of these problems, this hypothesis may remain untested for some time to come. (Webb and Cartwright, 1978, p. 244)

The hypothesis that dreams function to assimilate anxiety so that individuals can cope better in their waking life has been tested by Greenberg, Pillard, and Pearlman (1972) and Grieser, Greenberg, and Harrison (1972). Their findings support the adaptive value of dreams and suggest that when dreaming is intact in normal persons, they are able to face emotionally upsetting waking situations more directly and calmly than when equal periods of non-REM sleep or waking are inserted.

Another study that supports the hypothesis that one function of dreams is to work through anxiety-producing situations is a study of three groups of pregnant women (Winget & Kapp, 1972). Those who had the most dreams on childbirth had the least prolonged labor. Women who delivered their babies in less than 10 hours had anxiety in over 80 percent of their dream reports, whereas women whose labor lasted longer than 20 hours showed anxiety in their dreams only 25 percent of the time. Women whose anxiety dream reports were between these two extremes had an average length of labor. It appears that the more the woman experiences the anxiety of childbirth in her dream, the more effective and relaxed she can be during the actual delivery. The findings support the adaptive value of dreams in assimilating anxiety.

Another study suggesting that dreams have an adaptive value in allowing the dreamer to deal with upsetting psychological issues was conducted by Cartwright, Lloyd, Knight, and Trenholme (1984), who studied for six nights in the sleep laboratory the sleep and dream patterns of twenty-nine 30- to 55-year-old females who were going through a divorce. The subjects were administered the Beck Depression Inventory and divided according to their scores on that test into a depressed group of 19 subjects and a nondepressed group of 10 subjects. The divorced subjects were compared to nine nondepressed married females with a mean age of 35 years for whom divorce had never been considered. There were observable differences in the dreams of the different groups of subjects. The depressed women rarely dealt with marital issue in their dreams. In addition, while the nondepressed divorced women frequently dreamed of themselves in the role of wives, the depressed women almost never dreamed of themselves in that role. The depressed women had less overall anxiety in their dreams and became less anxious as the night progressed. These findings indirectly support the view that dreams function as safety valves that allow the dreamer to deal with anxiety-provoking issues.

Van Bork (1982) also provides indirect support that anxiety dreams or nightmares are an attempt to cope with an emotionally laden situation. In attempting to answer the question of why one wakes up out of an anxiety dream, Van Bork examined the manifest content of survivors of the Holocaust and people who lived in Japanese camps on Java and Burma in World War II. In traumatic dreams, individuals generally woke up at the moment of the traumatic situation. In a traumatic dream, one often deals with the repetition of a past traumatic event. When this traumatic event was one in which the person had no control over the situation, the anxiety dream comes to an end at the very moment that his or her typical traumatic situation occurs in the dream. Van Bork concludes that when an anxiety dream brings an end to sleep, one can surmise that the patient was confronted with an insurmountable problem. When the patient awakens from the dream, it indicates that he or she is struggling with him- or herself on an unconscious level; when there is a deadlock, the patient awakens from sleep. Van Bork's findings and conclusions provide indirect support for the anxiety-assimilating functions of dreams.

The hypothesis that dreams may help individuals integrate aspects of their personalities receives some support in a study by Cartwright (1974b) that examined the effects of a conscious wish on dreams. Cartwright found that subjects who were instructed to wish during the sleep onset period to change some personality characteristic about which they were concerned more often dreamed that they were enjoying the quality and were content to keep it as a part of the image they had of themselves.

The hypothesis that dreams have an information processing function has also been studied in the laboratory. Dreaming has been described as

an information processing activity that functions to match new experience
with representations of past events already stored in long-term memory.
To test this, Palombo (1984) asked nine 31- to 52-year-old patients who
reported dreams in psychotherapy whether their dream imagery recalled
a specific event from early in their lives. Forty-six of fifty consecutively
reported that their dreams contained imagery that was associated with
early life events. In a later series of 34 dreams, subjects were not questioned about the past. The same subjects spontaneously recalled early
events represented in the dream imagery only 13 times. The findings of
this study cannot be integrated with either psychoanalytic theory, which
attributes the influence of past experience on dreams to repressed wishes
rather than to memories of actual events, or with a random neutral stimulation theory.

Methods of understanding and studying the language of dreams are important in testing hypotheses about dreams. Some progress has been made
in this area with the development of scales for studying dream content.
As noted previously, Hall and Van de Castle (1966) have devised scales
to analyze dream content. These included the scoring of emotions such
as anger, apprehension, happiness, sadness and confusion, as well as of
descriptive elements as color, size, and intensity. Hall and Van de Castle
also constructed scales to measure theoretical concepts such as morality
or regression. The authors also review some scales devised by others to
study dream content.

Krohn (1972) developed a thematic scale for the assessment of object
representations in the manifest content of dreams. Krohn sees the manifest dream as similar to a Rorschach response or an early memory. After
reviewing dreams from a variety of sources, Krohn found marked differences in the humanness, differentiation, and warmth of various patients'
dreams. There were also differences in how rich or impoverished the images were, and these seemed to correspond to the extent of maturity of
the patients. Based on these observations, Krohn developed the Object
Representation Scale for dreams, which assesses the degree to which people are experienced as whole, consistent, and separate entities. Krohn
(1972) and Krohn and Mayman (1974) then did a series of studies to estab-
lish the reliability and construct validity of the scale. They concluded that
the rating of object representation on the manifest content of dreams and
early memories seems to provide a pure measure of the validity of the patient's object relations.

Further research is clearly needed to test specific hypothesis from different psychological theories about dreaming. The development of measures, instruments, and methods for studying dream language in a scientific manner is a preliminary step in the testing of hypotheses.

STUDIES ON THE USE OF
DREAMS IN PSYCHOTHERAPY

What are the uses of dreams in psychotherapy? How valuable is dream analysis in helping clients make changes? Most of the reported research on the use of dreams in psychotherapy is descriptive and anecdotal, taking the form of clinical case histories. Although dreams are reported to reflect progress in therapy, no single laboratory study has been done to test this. In fact, there has been little use of the sleep laboratory in testing areas of application to psychotherapy.

As an example of anecdotal literature, Marriott (1980) describes the case of a 29-year-old woman who was able to successfully overcome an anxiety state that had been maintained for 13 years. Through the combination of hypnosis and subsequent dream work, the woman gained sufficient ego strength to deal with the repressed emotions underlying her fears.

Tihansky (1982) also discusses the case of a 59-year-old ummarried woman with a history of 24 years of gradually progressive arthritis that did not respond to traditional treatment. Hypnoanalysis and dream interpretation helped the patient realize the source of her physical symptoms. She recognized that she had assumed the identity of her passive mother and kept her anger and tension pent up, with a subsequent worsening of her physical problems. The insight gained through dream interpretation helped her express her feelings more directly and cure herself of the physical symptoms.

Sarlin (1984) reports on the use of dreams in psychotherapy with deaf patients. He presents four case histories of deaf patients between the ages of 16 and 45 for whom dream analysis was effective. These individuals were from a lower middle and lower class clinic population with severe psychopathology, ranging from personality disorders to acute psychotic disorders. His findings showed that the patients could be trained to increase their capacities for self-observation and self-reporting and to interpret their dreams meaningfully. Sarlin suggests that cognitive training of these patients helped them gain insight into unconscious conflicts, which resulted in better integration of personality and greater autonomy. It is noteworthy that the patients in this study who derived benefit from dreams in psychotherapy are not those typically associated with insight-oriented psychotherapy or dream analysis.

Makarić (1979) reports on the use of dreams with an alcoholic population, noting that alcoholics undergoing alcohol deprivation often have "infantile" dreams in which they attempt to gratify their thirst for alcohol. Makarić studied dreams of 100 alcoholic patients and found that 16 of the subjects had 36 dreams of an infantile type, whereas the rest either had adult type dreams or could not remember their dreams. Makarić states that the information obtained from dreams can have an important diagnostic value and can be used together with other relevant data to contribute to a more objective analysis of the patient. He further suggests that the data obtained from the dreams may serve a preventive function for relapse and suicides.

Kaplan, Saayman, and Faber (1981) have suggested that dreams may be useful diagnostic indicators in the assessment of family problem solving. They examined the use of nocturnal dream reports to diagnose patterns of family functioning among five families made up of 21 people. Two families undergoing family therapy comprised the treatment group, and three families drawn up from a population ranging from very disturbed to superior functioning made up the nontreatment group. In the study, the manifest content of dreams was analyzed both quantitatively and qualitatively. The dream researcher was blind to the case history, presenting problem, or progress in therapy; similarly, the dream content and the dream analysis were unknown to the family therapist. Each family was rated independently by the therapist and the dream researcher. The results showed impressive agreement between the two assessments, and problem areas, family transactions, and treatment outcome were correctly identified by the dream researcher. The authors conclude that dream content analysis reflects the problem areas encountered by a family system, and they emphasize the diagnostic value of dreams in family therapy.

Other authors have stressed the value of dreams in reflecting the patient's progress in therapy and signalling the need for termination. Cavenar and Nash (1976) presented four cases to demonstrate the value of dreams in signalling the time for termination in psychotherapy. According to them, dreams can signal that the parameters of termination have been met. These include structural changes in dreams, improvement of ego functioning, resolution of transference neurosis, and the absence of marked countertransference difficulties. In a later article, Cavenar and Spaulding (1978) provide two further illustrations of how dreams that signal termination can occur in therapy.

All of the previous studies have been descriptive, and none has made use of the sleep laboratory. Of course, one very practical problem is that most psychotherapists do not have ready access to a sleep laboratory. In addition, asking patients in psychotherapy to spend several nights in a laboratory to record their dreams may present a great deal of resistance. Whitman, Kramer, and Baldridge (1963) have used the sleep laboratory to help them test certain hypotheses in psychotherapy. They wanted to find out what selection factors determine which dreams are told and which are not in a psychotherapeutic setting. Two subjects, one male hospital patient and one female volunteer graduate student, slept overnight in a dream laboratory twice a week for 8 weeks. When REM activity indicated that the subject was dreaming, he or she was awakened after 5 minutes and asked to tell the dream and his or her associations to it to the experimenter. After the dream night, the subject was also interviewed by a psychiatrist, to whom his or her dreams were reported. The experimentally obtained dreams that had not been related to the psychiatrist were examined the next day. It was found that dreams that contained an attitude which the dreamer anticipated would bring a negative response from the psychiatrist were not recalled. For the male patient, these consisted of homosexual feelings; for the female subject, these initially involved sexuality and later a denial of dependency. The dynamic thematic content of the dreams apparently influenced which ones were recalled, suggesting that the dreamer at some level knows the meaning of his or her dream.

One of the few studies reporting the effects of psychotherapeutic events on the contents of monitored dreams has also made use of the sleep laboratory. In Hunter and Breger's study (cited in Jones, 1970), four experimental subjects were brought together with a therapist to form a "sensitivity-therapy" group, each subject serving as the focus of the group's interpretation for two nights in a row. After each session, the dreams of that subject were collected. Two control subjects on whom baseline dream data were obtained together with the experimental subjects underwent two additional nights of dream collection after collection of their baseline dreams. Dream reports of the experimental and control groups were then scored by independent raters. Results suggested that psychotherapeutic events influenced dream content. All of the dreams of the experimental subjects incorporated other members of the group and were related to the theme of the preceding therapy sessions.

Cartwright, Tipton, and Wicklund (1980) are those rare researchers who have done controlled studies using the sleep laboratory as an adjunct to psychotherapy. In attempting to tackle the high drop-out rate in psychotherapy, they selected 48 patients whom they considered to be poor risks for staying in treatment. All of these patients were offered a 2-week program to prepare them for treatment. Sixteen of those declined and went directly into therapy. The remaining thirty-two subjects were sleep monitored for 8 nights. Half of these were given access to their dreams by awakening them from REM sleep periods, whereas the other half were awakened as often from non-REM sleep. Each morning, the material of the night before was discussed with the subjects by the experimenter who took a nontherapeutic role. The effect of these discussions was measured on the drop-out rate, with the finding that those individuals who successfully retrieved and discussed dreams as opposed to material other than dreams stayed in psychotherapy at a significantly higher rate and also used the hours in therapy more productively.

The previous study is an example of how the sleep laboratory can be used to test the applications of dreams to psychotherapy. Although little systematic research under controlled conditions is being done in this area, the increasing and renewed interest in dreams will likely prompt further research along this line.

CONCLUSION

Research conducted so far on dreams has demonstrated a physiological basis for dreaming and has established that everyone dreams with nightly regularity. In spite of the difficulties associated with conducting dream research to correlate it with psychological events, studies suggest that there is a continuity between dreaming and waking phenomena and that dreams reflect waking concerns and styles. The research also suggests that dreams are influenced by waking conditions and are not just random, meaningless activity. In addition, it establishes that most individuals require a certain amount of dreaming and that dream deprivation can result in some psychological disturbances. Many studies have supported the view that dreams have an adaptive function as well. Very few experimental studies have been conducted to test different theories of dreaming, and the development of methods and measures for studying dream language is needed to test hypotheses from specific theories. Studies on the use of dreams in psychotherapy have been limited to descriptive and anecdotal case histories for the most part. Few researchers have done controlled studies on the use of dreams in psychotherapy using the sleep laboratory as an adjunct to psychotherapy. The one attempt in this area suggests that dreams can have an adaptive value in psychotherapy by preventing drop-outs and involving patients in their therapy. Research on dreams and psychotherapy is still in its infancy stages at this point.

Chapter 3
The Use of Dreams in Psychotherapy

> A dream which is not interpreted is like a letter
> which is not read.
>
> *The Talmud*

For many therapists, the terms *dream analysis* and *the unconscious* are generally associated with Freudian psychoanalysis. For some, these words conjure up images of fortune-telling and magic. With all the recent advances in new methods of changing people's behaviors, what place do dreams have in modern psychotherapy? What function can dreams serve at a time where there is growing emphasis on brief, practical, and goal-oriented psychotherapy with observable behavior changes?

One of the misconceptions about dream analysis is that it is an esoteric practice limited only to those intellectualized therapists and clients who take delight in analyzing and free-associating to their dream images. Jungian theory on archetypes reinforces this misconception. In reality, dream analysis can be one of the most efficient tools we have in psychotherapy. It can shorten the amount of time spent in therapy rather than prolong it, because through the interpretation of dreams a therapist can very quickly get to the crux of the client's problem. Dream analysis is also very practical and is focused on making behavioral changes. Following the interpretation of the dream, the client is asked how he or she can practically apply what has been learned.

Another misconception is that dream analysis and psychoanalysis are synonymous. Dreams were termed "the royal road to the unconscious" by Freud (1950), and dream interpretation has been an important part of psychoanalytic psychotherapy. However, as discussed in the previous chapter, dreams have been utilized by therapists who do not necessarily endorse a psychoanalytic orientation (Delaney, 1979; Faraday, 1974; Garfield, 1974; Perls, 1969; Rossi, 1972; Ullman & Zimmerman, 1979). In addition, dream interpretation can be combined with any number of theoretical approaches. Following the interpretation of a dream, the therapist can use a variety of techniques to apply the dream message to daily living. For example, a client who has a dream that highlights his or her lack of assertiveness can then engage in role play to rehearse difficult assertive situations. I have even on occasion used dream analysis in conjunction with a relatively structured behavioral approach for treating bulimia. While the client kept a binge diary of her thoughts and feelings prior to binge eating, she also recorded her dreams at the same time. For example, when the client's binge eating was related to her difficulty in heterosexual relationships, she reported such thoughts as "Why doesn't he call?" and "Why do I spend so much time thinking about him?", which directly preceded a binge. In her dreams, she saw men as "giants" or "celebrities," whom she put on a pedestal, and herself as a "lilliputian." Later dreams dealt with her relationship with her father, which contributed to her current difficulties with men. In this case, her dreams added a deeper dimension to treatment and brought out material that may not have been obtained otherwise. Thus, dream analysis is not restricted to a psychoanalytic orientation.

Another misconception about dream analysis is that its use is limited to bright, verbal, intellectual clients. While it is true that articulate clients, particularly those with self-awareness, will benefit from this mode of treatment, dream analysis can be used even with those clients who are neither very verbal nor psychologically oriented. For example, dreams can be used with both children and "acting-out" adolescents, as well as other client populations who are deemed inappropriate for insight-oriented psychotherapy.

Because of these misconceptions about dream analysis, many therapists have been reluctant to use it with their clients. However, even clinicians who do not share these misconceptions have not utilized dream interpretation in their practice as much as they could. The main reason has been that there is very little guidance for the interested clinician on how to approach dream interpretation. There is generally little formal training for psychotherapists in dream analysis. It is not taught as part of the graduate school curriculum and is barely touched upon in practicum courses in psychotherapy. There is also no textbook, handbook, or "how-to" literature that discusses dream interpretation in a simple step-by-step fashion for the clinician. Most of the books on dream interpretation are either Freudian or Jungian or only describe interpretation without clearly discussing how it is derived. Other books that may give some guidelines are intended for a general rather than a professional audience. Dream analysis is seen as an art by many people, and that may be partly responsible for the lack of explicit instruction in analyzing dreams. Dream analysis, like any other tool in psychotherapy, is partly an art and depends on the intuitiveness, skill, and experience of the psychotherapist. However, like any other therapeutic method, it can be approached systematically, and with practice, the clinician can become more comfortable and skilled with this important tool.

The opportunity for dream analysis in psychotherapy is always there. I remember my first day back at work after being at a dream analysis seminar. It appeared as though all the clients I saw that day were discussing their dreams, even new ones who had come for other reasons. I have had this experience when I have attended training workshops in other areas. After returning from a sexuality workshop, it appeared that most of my clients were discussing sexual issues, even those who had never broached the subject before. Why? Was it merely a coincidence? I think not. I think clients have always talked about sex or dreams or any other area. I had only become more conscious of these themes and was more attuned to openings.

How many times, for example, does a client come in, complaining about a bad night or bad dreams that kept him or her awake? How many times do therapists "tune out" what the client is saying and want to come to the "real issue"? How often do therapists ask, directly or indirectly, about dreams? The material for dream analysis is always there, ready to be explored. All the therapist has to do is to be attuned to it, to listen for it and, at times, to ask for it directly, because dreaming is a universal phenomenon. *We all dream.*

With whom does the therapist use dream analysis and when? Since all clients dream, a therapist can use it with anyone who comes for help and wants to better understand him- or herself. Dream therapy can be used all the time or intermittently, depending on several factors, including the client's willingness and ability to discuss dreams, the therapist's comfort with dream analysis, and the nature of the problem. Some analysts may maintain that there is no situation in which dream analysis is not relevant, even crises. However, each therapist must determine on a personal basis how much to utilize dream interpretation.

In my experience, I have found dream analysis to be one of the most useful tools in getting directly to the root of a person's conflicts. It has been particularly helpful with those clients who appear to have little or no insight into why they feel depressed or anxious. Frequently, people will come in for treatment because of symptoms they may be having, although they maintain that everything in their life seems to be going smoothly. They truly have no idea what is going on inside them. Dream analysis is particularly helpful for neurotic, repressed, intellectualized individuals and "cuts through the garbage" very quickly.

Dream analysis is one of the most efficient ways of bringing intrapsychic conflicts to the forefront. Frequently people act in neurotic and self-defeating ways because they are unaware of those unconscious conflicts that are contributing to their behaviors. Through the use of dreams, they can have an understanding of these unconscious conflicts and make conscious changes based on this understanding. Dream analysis can shorten the therapeutic process by helping to identify focal issues early in treatment.

Dreams are an excellent source of information that can be used to gain a diagnostic impression. The dream is often a reliable source of information because it is free from the conscious intent to blur the issue or to "look good." In addition to the diagnostic application, dreams also have a therapeutic value. Each dream provides a message for action that the client is more likely to act on because the wisdom comes from within.

Frequently people's dreams are an impetus for them to enter psychotherapy, even though they may not relate that except upon direct inquiry. I recall one client I had seen for psychotherapy for a period of several months. It was only toward the termination of treatment that she related the original dream that had driven her to seek help. She dreamed that she was on a boat, ready to jump off. The dream alerted her to her suicidal tendencies and served as a warning. She had known about these tendencies on a subconscious level for some time, but the dream brought this knowledge to the foreground and pushed her to action. This happens more frequently than we realize because therapists generally don't ask for this kind of information when they first see someone in treatment. They ask about thoughts, feelings, symptoms, behavior, but seldom about dreams, which can provide a wealth of information.

Sometimes clients may have dreams about the need for psychotherapy without being aware of it, as in the case of a woman who came for treatment at the insistence of her friend. Linda was a capable, self-sufficient woman who had always handled her problems by herself. In recent months, following a trip to her childhood home, she had become increasingly depressed and could not understand the reason for her depression or why she could not handle it on her own. She was filled with doubt about a decision she had to make and had finally made up her mind prior to coming in for treatment. She had resolved the conflict in her mind but decided to come for one session anyway, since she had already made an appointment. We had a pleasant meeting, talking about the crisis she had recently experienced and about the decision she had made. She related that she did not see a need for further therapy at this time, since she had already made a decision. The door was left open for her to come at a future date should she want to do so, with the suggestion that she bring in her dreams if and when she came again. At this point, she related a dream she had had that same morning:

> I am riding on my bicycle on the way back from a social event on a path I had driven on before. On the way back, the ground was overturned, and I fell in a hole. Workmen picked me up, but my bicycle was still in the hole. They were going to get the

trouble-shooter to get my bicycle out. I was still hanging, being held up by the work-men.

We interpreted the dream together. She is traveling on a familiar path (life), which has always been smooth in the past, but now "the ground is falling out from under her." Her inner drive (her "wheels") that had kept her going in the past is not functioning now. This refers to her depression. Her work ("workmen") has been holding her up (she had in fact been spending increasing time at work, which had been sustaining her) until she can get a "troubleshooter" who can help her to get on with life.

"What is a troubleshooter?" she was asked.

"Someone who solves problems."

"And who would help you solve the problem of getting back on with your life?"

She smiled, "A therapist."

The dream was indeed a message for her that she needed therapy. Although she had outwardly made a decision and consciously felt she had resolved her problem, she had not resolved the unconscious conflicts underlying her decision. Linda in fact returned for psychotherapy a year later, following a similar crisis, again precipitated by a trip to her childhood home. The major mode of treatment for her was dream analysis.

This is also an example of how interpretation of dreams can serve as a means of involving clients in therapy. Once a dream is interpreted and clients can see how much of the seemingly nonsensical material they bring in relates to their current difficulties, they will bring in more and more dreams. Many clients frequently have a dream the night preceding a therapy session. Frequently, they intuitively know its meaning.

The first dream in psychotherapy generally reflects the client's attitude about it, as in this one:

> *I was traveling on a bus through all the different places I had lived. The scenery shifted according to the different cities I had lived in during my life. Parts of the road were smoother than others. There did not appear to be anyone driving the bus. I got to my destination, an area I had never been to before. I was very, very thirsty.*

The dream depicted the dreamer's life so far, some parts of it smoother than others. The new destination never explored before was psychotherapy, and the dreamer was "thirsty" (eager) for it. The dream also has other components, including a bus with no driver. Future car dreams by this client could serve as a barometer of how much she is "in the driver's seat."

Dreams are like a progress report, an internal barometer of how the dreamer is doing, how he or she is progressing through the path of life. People frequently have dreams where they are driving some kind of vehicle. Are they just coasting? Are they going too fast? Too slow? Does it seem like a roller coaster at times? Are they letting someone else do their driving for them? At different phases of treatment, clients' dreams reflect the changes they are making in therapy and suggest directions in which to grow. Looking at a progression of dreams is watching someone's development in psychotherapy.

Julia, a young, attractive professional woman who had been married for a number of years, entered therapy when her old boyfriend came back into her life and wanted her to leave her husband. She was torn with doubt about what course to take, as she loved both of them. She was asked to have a dream about her decision, whereupon she had a dream that she saw Tony, her old boyfriend, wearing a sweater just like the one worn by one of the most obnoxious, devious men with whom she worked. In her dream, she subconsciously realized some of Tony's deviousness, which she had not consciously acknowledged. Tony subsequently confirmed this unpleasant side of himself in reality. Julia decided to remain with her husband, who was having a very difficult time dealing with the situation. In her next dream, Julia dreamed that her husband was going through an initiation ceremony, and she was standing by his side. This helped her realize that her husband was going through his own problems, independent of her, and that she needed to stand by and help him through the turmoil. Later dreams brought out some of the sources of stress in her marital relationship that had made her vulnerable to the advances of an old boyfriend. She dreamed that she knew that an intruder was coming into her bedroom but that her husband was ignoring what was happening despite her calls for help. This helped her become aware of her husband's ignoring the situation and her cries for help in working on their marriage. Subsequently, she dreamed that she had a minor infraction, and even though she had all the right papers to avoid being punished, she ended up in jail anyway. The feeling she had upon waking from this dream was similar to the one she experienced in the dream about her husband—that no matter what she did right, she would continue to be punished. Julia's dreams coincided with the stages that she was passing through in psychotherapy in dealing with her marital problems. They both reflected and illuminated the different phases she was experiencing in attempting to deal with her situation.

Julia's case illustrates how dreams generally get to the heart of the matter faster and more dramatically than other methods and save many psychotherapy sessions. Dreams can point the path to pursue in psychotherapy, with each ensuing dream possibly indicating a new direction. The therapist can be instrumental in directing the process of psychotherapy by suggesting that the client have dreams about certain areas. Frequently, the therapist can remove blocks to making changes by giving clients suggestions to have a dream about these blocks. For example, clients can be instructed to have a dream about their worst fears or about what is blocking them. Frequently, clients will arrive at an impasse in making changes. Dream analysis is helpful in illuminating the unconscious conflicts behind the impasse. When clients say they really do not know or do not understand why they are behaving in certain ways, the therapist can ask them to have a dream about it.

When clients are having difficulties in making decisions, a dream can be very illuminating. Laura separated from her husband after many years of marriage to help her decide whether she wanted to remain in the marriage. Her husband was pressuring her to reach a decision, and the conflict and ambivalence for her was becoming unbearable. Even though she reflected on this by herself and discussed the issues in therapy, she could not come to a decision. She was asked to have a dream about her marriage and reported dreaming that she was looking at a tiled kitchen floor with a big hole in it. She recalled thinking that she could not just put a patch on the hole because it would not fit, and people could fall over it and stub their toes. She would have to take out the whole floor. The dream was a powerful image, a reminder for her that she could not just "patch up" her marriage and go back to her husband as she had done for years.

Gina, who also separated from her husband and was having a difficult time deciding what to do, had this dream about her marital relationship:

My husband and I are driving down a road. We take a detour and are in the midst of some surrealistic, distorted trees, with all the branches cut off, all the life gone out of them, like they are ossified.

She recognized this as a powerful image for the route her marriage had taken. She realized that she and her husband had a distorted life-style and that all the life had gone out of their marriage.

Marsha, an attractive young woman who was trying to make a decision about whether to remain in her marriage or not, had a dream about a cat and a mouse who were playing games with each other. Her dream images succinctly described her marital relationship and the game of "cat and mouse" that she had been playing with her husband for a long time.

Dreams have very powerful imagery that can encapsulate issues more dramatically and simply than words. A dream image can express an idea in a picturesque manner, and this image can serve as an impetus for action. Nina had this dream about her work:

I am standing in my office, and there is a mongoose right under my skirt. It keeps irritating me, and I keep pushing it away. It is not really harmful, but it is such a nuisance to keep pushing it away.

This image described very dramatically the little nuisances she had to deal with daily at work. Although she could cope with them, they were irritating. The image spurred her to make a job change.

Dream images reflect the client's conflicts as well as the progress he or she is making in therapy. Besides serving as a mirror or barometer of the client's changes in therapy, dreams also reflect the client's feelings and expectations of therapy and comment on the therapist–client relationship. Dreams are an excellent way to understand and bring to the forefront the dreamer's expectations of therapy. It is important for the therapist to look for the client's attitudes about psychotherapy in dreams, because frequently clients may be unable to verbalize these feelings. In the dream referred to at the beginning of the chapter, for example, the client saw psychotherapy as "an area I have never been to before," and her attitude about it was one of eagerness ("I am very thirsty"). Another client saw therapy as "a place where I get all my needs met." This client's expectations of a magic cure or of therapy meeting all his needs without his needing to do anything himself was important to understand and explore with him before he could make any progress.

Janice, a young woman who had been in treatment for several months, related this dream to her therapist:

> I am sitting in your waiting room, waiting for our appointment, while you are seeing Mary (a co-worker she had referred for therapy). Your session goes on and on, and it cuts into my hour. You only have five minutes to see me, and then you give me my folder to take away, saying you won't see me any more.

Janice had referred a number of her friends for treatment and had an underlying fear that her therapist would no longer have any time for her. The dream was a good vehicle to bring these feelings, which might not have been verbalized otherwise, to the surface.

The client's attitudes about the therapist are also important to understand, because frequently the way the client deals with the therapist is how he or she relates to others. Transference is frequently shown in dreams, and the therapist needs to constantly look for the symbolic figures in dreams that hide this transference. For example, a therapist could be seen as a junk dealer by a client. This client's attitudes about the worth of therapy are clearly different from one who sees the therapist as a wise man or a magician. In the dream discussed earlier in this chapter, the therapist was seen as a troubleshooter. In this case, the client clearly saw the therapist as one who would troubleshoot with her and help her solve her problems herself, rather than one who would be providing her with answers. Other clients have used different symbols for therapists that have depicted their attitudes and expectations of therapy. Mike saw the therapist as an "aerobics instructor," which he defined as "someone who gets you in shape." Norman saw the therapist as a "masseuse" and therapy as a "massage parlor," where "it hurts at first but then you feel so good and relaxed afterwards." The way the therapist is seen reflects the unconscious attitudes of the client to treatment, and these need to be recognized and dealt with for progress to be made in therapy.

Frequently, the dreamer will have feelings about the therapist that he or she is unable to discuss. These may interfere with treatment unless they are brought out into the open. For example, a client may be unable or unwilling to express feelings about a therapist's nationality, skin color, or sex but may have a dream that brings these biases into the open. Norman had some feelings about his therapist's race and wondered if his therapist, who was of a different ethnic background, could understand him. He had a dream where he was talking to an Oriental woman who was unable to speak his language. The dream served as a vehicle to bring these feelings out into the open. Carey had a dream where he saw his psychotherapist sitting in his mother's chair. Again, the dream made it possible to discuss feelings that may not have come out otherwise or quite so clearly. Sometimes the therapist may be aware of feelings the client has about him or her but may not know how to elicit them, since bringing them into the open may result in denial or silence. For example, a client may have dreams about loss or separation and yet be unable to talk about these feelings in therapy and deal with termination issues. Dreams can pave the road for discussing these areas.

Dreams can also help the therapist clarify personal attitudes about his or her clients and work. For example, a therapist having difficulty relating to a certain client may see in dreams certain aspects of the client or him- or herself of which he or she has not been consciously aware. Colleen, a young psychotherapist, was puzzled by her increasingly angry feelings about her client until she had a dream where her client and Colleen's mother were incorporated into the same figure. Colleen was then able to understand and work through her own countertransference toward her client. Another therapist reported that she was spending more and more time and energy on one of her clients, which was draining her physically and emotionally. However, she continued to invest her energies in the client's daily crises until she had a dream that she was being sucked dry by a leech. The image helped her realize how much she was bring drained, and she was able to set some limits with her client.

Sometimes a dream may bring to the therapist's awareness some aspects of a client that he or she has not seen before, and this can help the therapist determine how to proceed in psychotherapy. A few months ago, I saw a young married woman in therapy and had an uneasy feeling about her. I could not quite put my finger on it, but I felt that we were not making contact and that she did not appear to understand what I was saying. The woman was a college graduate, and I did not feel that it was her intelligence that was at question. I had a dream about her the following night where she was an adolescent, and the very primitive, childlike features of her were highlighted in the dream, features that I had not seen consciously, particularly in view of her college degree and her marital status. I understood that the communication problem was because I was relating to her as a mature adult when emotionally she was a child. I was then able to tailor my approach to address the child in her.

Dreams can also clarify the therapist's attitudes about his or her work and can have a strong personal value. Several years ago, I was going through a very "lazy" period at work, which I did not pay particular attention to consciously until I had this dream:

> I am in my office, and I see fifteen cats lying on the bed. I ask my colleague if I should call security to chase them out, but he says he thinks I can chase them out myself.

The dream helped me become aware that I was "sleeping on the job," and I was able to identify fifteen variables that were contributing to my laziness. I also realized that I could probably deal with these myself, without seeking outside help.

Therapists have given numerous examples where they have used dreams to help them work on difficult situations in psychotherapy, in their jobs, or in their personal lives, which directly or indirectly affect their work with clients. Psychotherapists can deepen their understanding of themselves and their clients by paying more attention to their dreams and acting upon them. Therapists, just like their clients, can learn to "sleep on a problem" and utilize this very important tool in both their professional and personal lives.

Of course, dream analysis has a very important personal value for the client in treatment. Most people coming for treatment can benefit from it, but it is particularly helpful for those intellectualized clients who can analyze their problems at length and offer many hypotheses but have no real insight into their self-defeating behavior. Laura, a particularly attractive young woman who was intelligent, warm, witty, creative, and had many other positive attributes besides, related that more than anything else, she wanted to be married and have children. However, in nearly 8 years she had not had more than a casual relationship. The problem wasn't a lack of opportunities to meet men, because she met many in the course of her daily life. She had thought about this problem for many years, had discussed it with others, and had a great deal of anxiety about it. It was suggested that she have a dream about what got in her way of a committed relationship. She came in the next session and said, "I think it's my ego." She recalled this dream:

> I am in a hospital where Jim, a man whom I had gotten close to and who had abruptly withdrawn from the relationship, was busy treating patients or something. I am tired of waiting and get angry and leave. He is hurt but so am I.

Laura interpreted this dream to mean that her pride and ego got in the way, that she expects a great deal from men, and interprets their genuinely being busy as a rejection. This stemmed back to her childhood, when her mother had always been pampered by her father and had led Laura to believe that she had to play "hard to get" all the time. Following this dream, she worked on lowering her expectations in relationships and becoming more open with men. In this case, dream analysis helped to elucidate to Laura some of her behaviors that were contributing to her perceived rejection by men.

Another example of dream analysis helping the intellectualized client is the case of Tom, a young, personable, verbal attorney who came to therapy because he was having anxiety attacks and could not understand the reasons for them. After a couple of therapy sessions, which were pleasant, intellectualized, and superficial, he had a dream that he "was not doing his homework." He related this to what had been happening in therapy so far—that he was not getting down to the basics. He had another dream in which he had to dig into the roots of the house where he had been raised in order to lay a solid foundation. After this dream he realized that he was only dealing with superficial issues in therapy and that to "get down to the roots," he had to go back to the "house where he was raised" (his childhood). The next dreams brought out long-standing unconscious feelings about his father that were coming to the forefront at this point in his life and causing much conflict.

Dream analysis is not limited to the verbal client. It is also very helpful for the nonverbal, blocked client. Jane came in for therapy feeling quite depressed and had tremendous difficulty talking about what was bothering her. She related that she felt blocked and did not appear to be achieving her full potential. Further questioning did not elucidate what was blocking her. It was suggested that she have a dream to find out what was getting in her way of achieving her potential. In the following session, she related this dream:

> I am trying to get a friend out of jail but before I can do that I have to go through several churches with my parents. There's one in North Mountain Park where they have that crazy dude dunking others. It's a real farce.

Jane related her religious background. She was brought up as a strict Catholic but was no longer practicing the religion. This dream revealed that part of Jane was "locked up." She doesn't let herself do what she wants because of religious values which in reality she describes as a "farce" or absurd. Although Jane had a boyfriend whom she had loved for the past eight years, she had let her guilt about her parents' values, which she no longer believed in, keep her from moving in with him. Following this dream, Jane became consciously aware of this conflict and was able to deal with it. Further dreams illuminated other blocks that kept her from her achieving her full potential.

Dream analysis is not restricted to adults; in fact, it can be particularly helpful with adolescents and children, even those who are not very verbal. Adolescents' dreams frequently pinpoint the core problem in therapy. For example, David, a teenage boy, was referred by the Juvenile Court for acting-out behavior. In therapy, he related that he had moved out of his mother's house since his parents' divorce and was living with his paternal grandmother. He spent most of his therapy sessions venting his hatred and anger toward his mother in an excessive, obsessive manner. He saw his mother in only negative terms and could not acknowledge that she really cared for him. David's therapist had talked to the mother and knew she really cared for her son. In addition, the therapist recognized the ambivalence beneath the anger and attempted to help David integrate positive and negative aspects of his mother. Toward the end of treatment, David had this dream:

> I invite my mother to my graduation from high school. She comes to the graduation but I do not see her.

In the dream, David recognizes both his wish to have his mother at an important event in his life as well as the fact that *she cares but he does not see it*. He may even be rehearsing a future date when they might reconcile—at his graduation (from therapy? from childhood? from high school?). All of these elements provide rich material for psychotherapy. The dream encapsulates, in a very efficient and dramatic fashion, the main issue. It comes to the heart of the matter directly and weeds out irrelevant data. What is noteworthy about this example is that this was a relatively simple, nonverbal adolescent who would not be described as psychologically sophisticated and who frequently responded in monosyllables.

Younger children benefit from dream analysis as well. Ten-year-old Clara had a nightmare that she was being chased by a shadow while she was out on her paper route. She dreamed that although she did not wish to go out by herself at night, she felt that she had to because her parents wanted her to make money. Clara's father had recently gotten a decrease in his salary. Although the parents had not discussed their financial concerns with Clara, she had apparently sensed the situation and reflected her anxieties about it in her dream. The dream was a vehicle to bring her fears out into the open and discuss them with her family.

Dream analysis can also be used in working with couples. Greta and John were in marital counseling because of Greta's need for constant reassurance from John that he loved her. John had been involved in an affair that was terminated many years ago. To all outward appearances, he was now a loving, attentive husband. Both Greta and John affirmed that there was no reason for Greta's jealousy and constant need for reassurance, that John was supportive, and that Greta needed to become less dependent and insecure. Greta could not verbalize anything that her husband was overtly doing that was bringing on her feelings of insecurity, which only served to reinforce her feelings of inadequacy. During the course of therapy, she had this dream:

> I am hanging from the ceiling. My husband is talking to another woman. I keep trying to get his attention but he ignores me and can't hear me.

In her dream, Greta's unconscious acknowledged what she had not been able to consciously—that although her husband was not doing anything overtly to elicit her feelings of insecurity, that *by ignoring her, he left her hanging*. This dream brought to the surface the pattern of interaction between the couple that was not apparent outwardly, either to them or to the therapist.

Dream analysis is not limited to outpatient settings. It is very effective for night personnel in inpatient settings as well. Psychiatric nurses on the night shift have a unique opportunity to work with patients who are having dreams or nightmares and who may wake up with these dreams. These dreams can be significant in helping patients with their immediate problems and reinforcing their treatment. John, a patient in a drug detoxification unit, had a dream from which he woke up in a frightened state. He dreamed that he was headless and that the other patients on his ward were also without heads. Dream interpretation helped clarify the message of the dream for him. He realized that the missing heads represented the effects that cocaine was having on him, in that he was losing some of his abilities to think clearly. The dream was utilized effectively to strengthen his motivation for treatment.

Jerry was another young man for whom dream analysis was helpful in an inpatient setting. Jerry had been seeing his therapist for a number of months but was fairly resistant to bringing in dreams. He was hospitalized for depression eventually, and his therapist was contacted when Jerry woke up from a dream that was very upsetting to him. He was in a very agitated state, and the staff was concerned about him. The therapist started to question him calmly about the different features in his dream, and to the therapist's surprise, Jerry answered the questions instead of displaying his usual resistance. The dream depicted the core conflict in Jerry's life and outlined the issues he needed to discuss in therapy.

Dreams are important in all phases of therapy. Not only do they point out the direction in which therapy is going, they also signal when the client is ready to terminate. The client who had originally come for treatment because of a dream alerting her to suicidal tendencies had this dream after a few months of treatment:

I am climbing a mountain in the winter. I am unable to do it. I am able to climb this same mountain in the summer.

The dream highlighted the contrast between the past and the present. The change in weather reflected her internal changes (from depressed to happy) and how she was able to cope with the same problems under new conditions. The dream served as a signal that she was able to cope and was ready to end treatment, which she did after two sessions. On her last session, she had a dream that she was ready to leave "the cave where she lived." She alluded to the "underground where I explore" (psychotherapy where she had explored her thoughts and feelings), which had been "fun and yet scary."

CONCLUSION

Dreams are useful in all phases of therapy. They bring to the surface clients' expectations of therapy, highlight their progress, and signal the direction for further therapy sessions. They encapsulate, in vivid imagery, dramatically and briefly, the essence of the problem, and they "cut through the garbage" in getting to the core conflict in therapy. They serve as a barometer of client progress and also signal when it is time to end treatment. Rosenthal (1978b) stated that the decision to terminate depends on three judges: the analyst, the patient, and the dream. The most reliable and unbiased judge is the dream.

Chapter 4
Dream Theory

Dreams are subconscious truths.
M. S. Michel, *Sweet Murder*

Dreaming is a universal phenomenon, and research has established that we dream about four or five times during the night. It has been estimated the average adult spends an hour and a half nightly dreaming or *four years of his or her life* in the dream state (Garfield, 1974, p. 3). In spite of the vast amount of time we spend dreaming, many people have ignored this aspect of consciousness, simply because they do not understand it. Many clinicians have avoided looking at this part of human behavior because it does not make sense on the surface. Many times the dream may seem so nonsensical that we disown it as though it were not a part of us. However, we need to constantly remind ourselves that *we produce our dreams,* we create our dream figures and our dream stories, and to ignore our dreams is to ignore a whole aspect of personality or consciousness.

Dreams can be viewed as our friends, our allies, a source of enormous wealth that we can tap into to learn about ourselves. How many times do we hear the expression "Let me sleep on it"? How many times, as we are struggling with a problem, do we see a solution when we tap into that other level of functioning? Dreams are an enormous source of wisdom, and unlike other sources, they come directly from us. Clients in psychotherapy can learn to use their own internal wisdom, their inner guide, to learn about themselves. As Hall stated:

> If he [the patient] would give as much thought to himself during the day as he does during the night, man might deepen his self-knowledge to the point where he could master his conflicts instead of being mastered by them. For it is only be being completely self-conscious that man can be rational and wise in all of his undertakings. (1953, p. 234)

The view of dreams presented in this chapter is adapted from Hattie Rosenthal's theory of dream analysis (Rosenthal, 1980). As noted previously, although her training was primarily psychoanalytic, her method of interpretation is compatible with a number of theoretical orientations. The theory, as presented here, is adapted for the nonanalytic clinician.

According to Hattie Rosenthal, as we go about our daily lives, we have a number of thoughts, feelings, impressions, and ideas that we do not always process during the day. The dream material consists of those feelings, thoughts, and impulses that are not immediately available to consciousness. These are either unacceptable to us or unavailable at our conscious level of awareness. Psychoanalytic theory discusses the transfer of unacceptable material into the unconscious through repression. Many clinicians are comfortable with the use of the term *unconscious* and generally think of it as a "place" where repressed feelings are stored. Others prefer to talk about different levels of consciousness or awareness. When the terms *conscious, subconscious,* or *unconscious* are used in this book, they refer primarily to different levels of awareness and do not necessarily have all of the psychoanalytic implications that these terms often connote. The dream material thus is comprised of those thoughts and feelings that we may not be aware of in our waking state. Sometimes the dream material consists of thoughts and feelings that we already know, but the dream may magnify those in order to bring them closer to our attention.

One of the most important characteristics of dreams is their quality of profound honesty. In dreams, people depict themselves *as they are*, not as they would like to be seen, without the social masks of waking life and psychological defenses. Dreamers can choose to understand themselves by understanding their dreams or they can choose to ignore this self-knowledge.

Freudian theory has generally emphasized the baser, unacceptable impulses in dreams. Dreams, however, also depict our positive and creative energies, and unfortunately, little attention has been paid to those positive and often unrecognized potentials. There are numerous examples of people writing books, composing poetry, or even creating inventions after seeing the original idea in a dream (Delaney, 1985).

These positive impulses are not only reflected in inventions or poetry. Many people frequently dream of themselves behaving in a manner that they were not aware was possible for them. Bill, for example, always had a fear of speaking in public and did not feel he could make a speech in front of a group. In his dream, he saw himself speaking in front of a large audience and was surprised at his poise and confidence. The dream highlighted for him qualities that he did not think he possessed. Bonnie viewed herself as a fat, dumpy individual, and although she worked on improving her body image, she was unable to feel better about her body. In her dreams, however, she was looking at a photo of herself or walking into a room and felt positive about her body. The dreams helped her realize that she was capable of accepting her body. Clients frequently report dreams in which they behave assertively or confront an individual or situation that they did not feel they were capable of handling. These dreams help alert them to the strengths within themselves of which they were not aware. Frequently, dreams of this sort are a rehearsal for future behavior.

Dreams have another important function in regulating our affect mechanism. Through our dreams, we can discharge many unpleasant and unacceptable feelings. Dreaming is a way of releasing emotions, and by ventilating these, we do not have to act them out. As Rosenthal (1978b) stated, we can kill and not be sentenced for murder. She frequently congratulated her clients who reported a nightmare, by saying: "You have carried a nightmare within you for quite some time. Now you have the courage to face it. Congratulations!" Rosenthal found this function of dreams so important that she believed that without relief of these emotions in dreams, a volcano-type eruption may occur in the waking life. She regarded the dream as a means of both releasing and integrating unacceptable emotions.

The content of dreams varies from person to person and generally reflects the dreamer's culture and interests. We dream of people we know and environments of which we are familiar. A doctor may dream of stethoscopes, whereas a musician may dream of musical instruments. Children may dream of cartoon characters, whereas adults may dream of public figures that are part of their general milieu. Similarly, people of different cultures may use different symbols. A European therapist commented on the number of dreams that Americans have that involve driving some kind of vehicle and wondered whether Europeans who did not drive so much would have so many dreams about automobiles. Although each individual depicts and experiences his or her problems in a unique way, the commonality in dreams is that the basic conflicts are all human.

Dreams also vary in length, ranging from a brief image to a long, complicated dream. Short dreams generally focus on basic issues and lead to awareness and insight. A short dream encapsulates the focal issue without too many details or distractions. Long dreams, on the other hand, may hide the basic conflict and detract from the central issue. In a long dream, the focus is usually diverted to several issues, and the therapist or client may miss the central theme. Frequently, as clients become more involved in psychotherapy, their dreams become shorter and more focused on the central issue.

Like Jung, Adler, Perls, and others, Rosenthal believed that every dream has a message. The message comes in an obscure form so that the dreamer can decide whether he or she wants to understand it. Rosenthal disputed Freud's view that dreams are mainly a form of wish fulfillment, believing that we can generally get our wish fulfillment met in daydreams. Dreams tell us *what we do not know* or highlight what we already know at some level to magnify its importance and call it to our attention. The message is basically one from us to ourselves, telling us what we do not know and signalling a direction for action. The language of the message is at times obscure, but we can learn to understand it.

Dream language is like a foreign language, and dream interpretation is essentially translating this foreign language. In dream analysis, we are translating from one level of consciousness to another. The unconscious material before translation is termed the *latent* dream content, and the manner in which it emerges into consciousness is called the *manifest* dream content. The manifest dream content is the dream itself; the latent is its underlying meaning. Interpretation of dreams involves translating the obscure, latent content into intelligible meaning. The dream message comes in an unintelligible or disguised form so that the dreamer can have a choice whether he or she wants to decipher the message and bring it to a conscious level of awareness or to ignore it. Frequently, people are fearful of uncovering unconscious conflicts and having to deal with them. They choose to ignore the dream message and not to bring it to their consciousness.

It is interesting to note that the more ready one is to look at and deal with unconscious conflicts, the more similar the latent and manifest levels become. As people progress in therapy, their dreams become shorter and less obscure, and the manifest content is not very far removed from its latent, unconscious meaning. There is less need for translation and deciphering, and the dream message is frequently conveyed in a clear, unobscured fashion.

How does one go about translating from one level of consciousness to another? The therapist cannot interpret a dream immediately simply by listening to it. Dream interpretation needs thorough and comprehensive analysis, and like any other tool in psychotherapy, it needs to be learned accurately and patiently. It is tempting at times to provide superficial or premature analysis. This can do more harm than good, as the therapist may be providing an incorrect and arbitrary interpretation. It is important for the therapist to learn the alphabet of dream analysis first before attempting to decipher the foreign language of dreams.

Of what does this foreign language consist? Dream language is essentially pictorial language. We use pictures and images to depict ideas and feelings. The alphabet of dreams is made up of symbols, and in dream analysis, we translate these symbols to their original referrants. A symbol is something representing something else, which shares a common denominator with it. For an object to qualify as a symbol for another object, it must share common characteristics with it; otherwise, the interpretation would be an arbitrary one. To arrive at these common characteristics, the therapist needs to see what a particular symbol means to the dreamer. This can be done by looking at the visual metaphors in dreams.

In dreams we describe something abstract by describing something else that conveys the same feelings or has the same characteristics.

According to Rosenthal, symbols are individual and not universal. The same symbol could mean different things to different people. In a class of nearly thirty people, I asked each person to define a snake and got thirty different definitions. Several clients have reported dreams about cats. One individual saw them as "independent creatures," another as "parasites," and a third as "catty and vicious." The individuality of symbols is a very important point and needs to be emphasized. Rosenthal felt that the blind use of stereotypic symbols did an injustice to the dreamer's individuality. To give clichéd interpretations is to ignore the dreamer's unique qualities and experiences. Dream symbols originate from the specific history and life experiences of each individual, and it is only from this history that the therapist can interpret the meaning of the dreamer's symbols.

This view of symbols being individual to the dreamer and not universal is in direct contrast to Freud's view that everything in a dream stands for either a penis or a vagina. Symbols are not exclusively sexual, and to reduce all of our experiences to sexual ones excludes many other aspects of our total being. Rosenthal believed that had Freud lived longer, he would have revised this view himself. A sexual image does not necessarily stand for a sexual conflict. For example, many individuals have reported dreaming about snakes. Along with the clichéd interpretation of a snake standing for the male organ, a snake has also served as a symbol of creativity, deviousness, or danger for different dreamers. Even dreams that are sexual on the surface may not have a sexual meaning. Nancy, for example, reported an exciting sexual dream:

> I am in a "ménage-a-trois" with my husband and another woman, and I am enjoying the sex acts tremendously. I tell myself that if I just relax, I will have an orgasm.

When asked to define "ménage-a-trois," Nancy responded, "A sexual relationship between three people" and then smiled when she realized that the dream was about herself, her husband, and "the other woman." Nancy was separated from her husband, and he was having difficulty letting go of an affair he'd had and making a commitment to the marital relationship. Nancy was undecided whether she should press the issue and force her husband to make a decision. Her dream was telling her that if she relaxed and didn't push the issue, she would get some resolution.

Since symbols are specific to the dreamer, a therapist cannot interpret a dream without the client. Dream interpretation requires an intensive cooperative effort between therapist and client. The therapist uses skills, and the dreamer his or her associations to arrive at the dream's meaning. Dream analysis is a collaboration between therapist and client to understand the language of the dream. Cooperativeness between therapist and client is an essential component of dream analysis, and dream interpretation fosters client activity and initiation.

Dream language is made up of symbols that are individual to the dreamer and that have a common denominator with the object to which they refer. These symbols are by necessity concrete pictures, as we cannot dream in the abstract. Instead of dreaming about marriage, we may dream of a wedding band or a wedding ceremony. Instead of dreaming about our childish parts, we may dream of a child. We use pictures to stand for our ideas in the dream. Dream symbols are subjective abstractions of qualities and characteristics that are verbally communicated in the waking state. They are the nonverbal, pictorial representation of a quality, trait, or feeling.

Similarly, we do not dream about feelings in the abstract; we experience them instead. For example, we do not dream about fear, love, or hate—we *feel* these emotions. We may have dreams where we are naked and feel exposed or vulnerable or where we cannot get to our destination and feel frustrated. In all these dreams, we experience those emotions. The dream language is made up of pictures, events, and experiences that stand for our thoughts, feelings, and ideas.

Everything in a dream is symbolic. Not only are the different *objects* in the dream symbolic, so are the *actions*. For example, a woman dreaming that she fell in a hole could be referring to her depression, another dreaming that she is unable to put on the brakes in her car could be referring to her lack of control, and so on. Frequently, people report dreaming that they were warm, cold, hungry, or thirsty. Again, these could be symbolic of the cold or warmth they feel in their relationships, their hunger for affection, or their thirst for knowledge. Similarly, dreaming of climbing a mountain could stand for attaining a goal, and going up and down could refer to changes in moods.

In dream analysis, we translate the actions and objects and use them to build a dream story. If the dream is composed of symbols, and if every action and object in a dream is symbolic, then it is important to go through *everything* in a dream analysis. Every detail is relevant in dreams, no matter how unimportant it may seem at first glance—*otherwise we would not dream it*. This point cannot be understated. Every detail in a dream is noteworthy, and the psychotherapist needs to be thorough and exact in conducting dream interpretation. Just because a detail doesn't seem to fit or appears to be minor doesn't mean it should be overlooked. Sometimes, it may be that very detail that provides a clue to the dream. Although some therapists may not go into extensive interpretation in the interest of time, interpreting a dream patiently and thoroughly can be time saving in the long run.

If we cannot interpret every symbol in a dream, it is better to leave the dream partially interpreted than to prematurely or superficially provide an interpretation. It is important to remember that even if only part of a dream is interpreted, the client gets something from it. Frequently, another dream or further thought can help the client clarify its meaning later on.

Of course, all dreams directly concern the dreamer. This point is obvious but needs to be emphasized to serve as a reminder to the client and therapist when doing dream interpretation. Clients integrate their own unique experiences in dreams to provide themselves with a message for action. Every dream has a protagonist, the dreamer, and even though the manifest dream content may focus on other characters and events, it is important to ask why the dreamer is having certain dreams and why at this particular point in his or her life. Frequently, clients may dream about different people who may represent different aspects of their personalities, or they may dream about a situation outside themselves to give a message to *themselves* about that particular person or event.

Dreams are frequently a microcosm of life, and the action taking place in dreams may reflect the actions in waking life. For example, an indecisive woman may dream that she has to make a choice about what to buy but ends up with nothing, because she cannot make up her mind. A woman who feels shut off from her family may dream that she is sitting in a corner of the house by herself while the rest of the family is congregating in the living room. A procrastinator may dream that she is taking so long to get ready that she misses the bus. Frequently, when clients are asked if they see any relationship between the action in their dreams and what is going on in their waking life, they will respond, "That is the story of my life!"

Another aspect of dream language is the use of metaphor. Again, pictures are used to depict certain images. For example, Betty dreamed that she was wearing watches on her feet as she was running and knew that she was "running out of time." Linda dreamed that she could not fit into her boots and realized that she was "getting too big for her britches." Linda had another dream where her head was disproportionately large for the rest of her body and related that to her recent "big-headedness." Jane dreamed that her friend was handing her some "baloney" to make a meat loaf, which made her more cognizant of feelings she had about her friend. Similarly, puns and plays on words are all characteristics of dream language, and the therapist should frequently look for these in client's dreams.

These examples illustrate some of the processes that transform the latent content of dreams into new meaning. There are a number of dream mechanisms that characterize dream language, and some of these will be elaborated in a later chapter to help the therapist conducting dream interpretation. Dream language has its own rules of logic, which do not follow the rules of everyday conscious language.

CONCLUSION

Dreams consist of thoughts, feelings, and impressions that are not immediately available to conscious awareness. Although clinicians have emphasized the unacceptable impulses found in dreams, dreams also exhibit positive, unrecognized talents and potentials. Each dream conveys a message that comes in disguised form so that the dreamer can decide whether he or she wants to interpret it. Dream interpretation is translating from one level of consciousness to another. It consists of translating the manifest content of dreams (the story we see on the surface) into its latent meaning. A number of processes called dream mechanisms intervene between one level of consciousness and another. Dream language is like a foreign language, with its own rules of logic, and it is important to learn the fundamentals of this language first, patiently, thoroughly, and in depth. Dream language consists of symbols that share common characteristics with the object they represent. These symbols are individual and not universal, and thus dream interpretation is a joint collaboration between therapist and client. Symbols are concrete pictures, and both the actions and the objects in dreams are symbolic. Since everything in a dream is symbolic, the therapist doing dream interpretation needs to be thorough and not overlook details. All dreams directly concern the dreamer, and they are frequently a microcosm of life.

Chapter 5
Presenting Dream Analysis to the Client

You might as well hunt half a day for a forgotten dream.

Wordsworth, *Hart-Leap Well*

The true art of memory is the art of attention.

Samuel Johnson, *The Idler*

Before getting to the fundamentals of dream interpretation, it is important to discuss how to introduce dream analysis to clients so that they will bring dreams to therapy. The first step for the therapist is to educate clients about the importance of dreams and to encourage them to have dreams. As mentioned in the first chapter, clients may bring up the topic themselves, and the therapist needs to be attuned to openings. If they don't, the therapist can bring up the subject in the first session or after a few sessions with the client. A good time to introduce dreams to clients is generally at the first session, after the therapist and client have reached a mutual understanding of some of the problems and treatment goals.

A simple introduction to dream theory can follow. The therapist can tell the client that everyone dreams and that all of our dreams have meanings. Every dream has a message, and we can learn about ourselves from our dreams. The therapist can also tell the client that dreams are like a foreign language—they may seem nonsensical at first, but the message is there, in disguised form. In therapy, the client and therapist can decipher the message together and use it to achieve personal growth. The therapist can tell the client that dreams can speed up the therapy process by bringing conflicts to awareness sooner so that they can be resolved. In some cases, the therapist may recount a simple dream as an example and ask the client what he or she thinks of it. All of this is done to educate the client and spark his or her interest. In subsequent sessions, the therapist can further educate the client as they work on dreams together.

It is important to let the client know right away that the therapist cannot interpret a dream simply by hearing it, because the dreamer's symbols are strictly personal and cannot be interpreted without his or her cooperation. This not only allays the client's fears, but also emphasizes the cooperative and equal nature of the partnership, that the client and therapist are working *together* to help the client. This makes the client more involved and better able to take responsibility for his or her treatment. In addition, the client can be reminded that dream analysis is a valuable tool for self-discovery that can be used even after treatment is over.

After educating the client about the value of dreams and answering any questions, the therapist can then ask the client to record his or her dreams and bring them to the next session. The therapist can encourage the client to keep a note pad or small tape recorder by his or her bed and to write down or dictate dreams into the recorder immediately upon waking, since they tend to be forgotten very quickly. The therapist can encourage the client to concentrate on having a dream before going to bed; if the client is working on a specific problem in therapy, he or she can be instructed to have a dream about that particular issue.

Frequently, these instructions are sufficient for the client to recall and record dreams. In some situations, more specific hints for remembering dreams may be helpful. Gayle Delaney, in her book *Living Your Dreams* (1979, pp. 210–212), provides excellent suggestions for improving dream recall, and the therapist may wish to provide the client with copies of those instructions. The therapist can stress the importance of having paper and pen by the bed *before* going to sleep, which acts as a suggestion to recall a dream the next morning and also eliminates the necessity of searching for a paper and pencil upon awakening, as the dream may be lost to memory by the time writing utensils are found. Some clients may prefer the use of a tape recorder to talk into upon awakening, although this is not always feasible, particularly if there are others sleeping in the same room who may be disturbed. It may also be wise to have a small night light or flashlight by the bed to use to record the dream should one awaken in the middle of the night. Also available are pens with flashlights that may be useful for recording dreams at night, as well as writing pads with small lights attached.*

Patricia Garfield, in her book *Creative Dreaming* (1974, pp. 178–181), suggests another method for recording dreams without the use of a night light or without opening one's eyes. She suggests buying unlined 5" × 8" note pads that are sealed with string embedded in the plastic binding and a

---

*These "Nite Notes" can be ordered for $10.00 from Kier Concepts, Inc., P.O. Box 1731, La Mesa, California 92041.

high-quality ballpoint pen that writes easily. When she wakes up with a dream, she records it *with her eyes closed* in the following manner: She grasps the note pad with the 8″ side held horizontally with her left finger-tips. She braces the pad on the bed or night table beside her while lying on her left side or upon her chest while lying on her back. She holds the right hand in a normal writing position except that the little finger is extended upward in order to feel the top edge of the pad. She then writes the dream across the pad making the line straight by feeling the top edge of the pad as a guide. When she arrives at the end of a line, she lowers her left-hand fingertips to indicate the starting position of the next line and returns the pen in her right hand to the spot marked by her left finger-tips by tactual contact. She likens this to a typewriter carriage returning to the next line. Keeping the little finger extended while writing corrects for the tendency to write in a downward curve in the dark. After she fills one page with writing, she turns the page, presses it flat, and continues the same process, using both sides of the paper, until she completes writing the dream. The client who does not wish to open his or her eyes or turn on the lights can practice writing with closed eyes using this method before using it to record dreams.

Besides having writing or recording equipment by the bedside, clients may wish to use other techniques to help them recall dreams. Some individuals have reported having a glass of water by the bedside and drinking half of it before going to sleep. They then make the posthypnotic suggestion to themselves to recall the dream when they drink the other half upon awakening. In addition to visual reminders, the self-suggestion to remember a dream upon awakening is most important. It is no coincidence that many clients frequently recall dreams they had the night before their therapy session.

Going to bed with a clear mind is also conducive to dream recall. Fatigue, drugs, alcohol, sleeping pills, and certain prescription drugs may have an inhibiting effect on the recall of dreams. The mind needs to be clear of external factors. Sometimes reviewing the events of the day before falling asleep can result in a clear head for a dream that night.

Dreams are fragile and can be lost to memory unless they are recalled and recorded immediately. Even when a dream is clear in a person's mind, and he or she has rehearsed and memorized it with the intention of writing it down later after awakening, all too often it is completely lost the next morning. Because of this, it is important for the dreamer to allow some quiet time upon awakening to remember and record dreams. Sometimes an alarm clock or even the act of opening one's eyes may destroy the dream memory. Some clients may wish to recall their dreams on weekends when they spontaneously get up and do not have to use an alarm clock. Others can teach themselves to wake up without an alarm clock or music. When awakening from a dream, the dreamer can remain with his or her eyes closed and recall the dream; sometimes the dreamer needs to think backwards to feel his or her way back into the dream state. If only a part of a dream is clear, the dreamer should relax and slowly think backwards in order to recall the rest of the dream. On some occasions, changing positions may help facilitate dream recall, since getting into the body position in which the dreamer had the dream may facilitate the recall of other aspects of the dream.

The therapist should remind the client to record dreams, even if only a fragment or an image is recalled. Many times the act of recording part of a dream will elicit the rest of it. Occasionally clients make judgments about dreams immediately upon waking up, labeling them silly, irrelevant, or unimportant. The time to interpret a dream and determine its importance is later, after recording it. At times clients may realize that the fragment or image they felt was unimportant was in reality the whole dream.

As discussed in an earlier chapter, the shorter the dream is, the more likely it is to focus on basic conflicts and to hide the issue. Gina, for example, frequently could recall brief images upon awakening. One night she went to sleep holding on to her pillow, and to her surprise and horror, it turned into an old, rotting, gnarled piece of wood. As she described something that was cuddly and gave comfort turning into something old, wrinkled, and gnarled, she started to cry, realizing that she was dreaming about her dying grandmother who had "shriveled up."

People frequently report that they are surprised when they reread a dream that they had written a day or two before that they have almost no recollection of it. Dreams are very fragile and fleeting, just like thoughts, and the client needs to learn to hold fast to them and record them before they disappear from memory.

Sometimes the client may wish to have a dream on a particular topic, a process called dream incubation. The client can make a self-suggestion before going to sleep to have a dream about a particular area of concern. Frequently, the therapist can make a suggestion to the client to have dreams about certain areas that he or she is working on in therapy. For example, a client may wish to have a dream about a relationship with the opposite sex, or about parents, work, or any number of conflictual areas. Carey, for example, was having a difficult time dealing with his feelings about his mother. He hated her for no apparent conscious reason and could not understand his feelings toward her. His attitude toward his mother also interfered with his current relationships. He had a dream where he was surprised by the amount of love he felt for his mother, feelings he had repressed years ago following what he perceived as her desertion of him. He had buried these feelings and started to hate her and see her only in negative terms; similarly, he tended to see his current relationships with women in black and white terms. The dream helped him integrate positive and negative feelings toward his mother and to see her and other women more realistically.

Clients can incubate dreams on a number of areas, dealing with whatever issues they may be working on in therapy. Although most of the time, the simple suggestion before falling asleep to have a dream about a particular topic is sufficient, other techniques can facilitate dreams about specific problem areas. Gayle Delaney (1979, pp. 217–219) offers very helpful step-by-step suggestions for incubating a dream. For the client who would like to incubate a dream about a specific question, Delaney offers some hints. She suggests that he or she record what the day was like before going to sleep. The client can review these thoughts, feelings, and actions during the day. After recording thoughts and feelings during the day, the client may wish to write down a discussion of the problem or question that he or she wants to dream about. This helps put the client in the frame of mind where he or she is receptive to the dream and consciously thinking about his or her problems. Following the incubation discussion, the client can write a one-line question or request that best expresses the issue about which he or she wants to dream. For example, Lester's incubation question was, ''Why am I procrastinating about retiring?'' John asked himself, ''What is blocking me from going to school?'' Sometimes a previous dream can suggest an incubation question. Len had a dream where he was told that he had three problems. He could only figure out two of those in his first dream. The next night he asked himself ''What is the third problem I need to work on?'' Repeating a phrase over and over before falling asleep generally brings a dream on that topic. Delaney's method for incubating a dream is a successful one and makes a great deal of sense. Frequently, we dream about what we are thinking of prior to falling asleep. Her method more or less ensures that the last thought we have is what we want to dream about.

It is important to think through the incubation phrase or question thoroughly before asking it. Dreams can not supply us with information that we do not know, or we could be asking ourselves questions such as ''What is the winning number in this month's lottery?'' Incubation is also not a gimmick to get quick answers or an excuse for not thinking through problems. Frequently, when we ask inappropriate questions, the dream may surprise us with its answer. A student who was nowhere near formulating a dissertation topic asked himself, ''What should my doctoral question be?'' The dream, cleverly enough, did not provide him with a simple answer, but answered a question about appropriate doctoral behavior. Mary, who was not recalling her dreams despite various suggestions to herself, harshly told herself, ''You *will* have a dream tonight!'' She had a dream where she was placing excessive pressure on herself. Her dream was in effect telling her to stop being so hard on herself. The dream question needs to be asked with care, and the answers may be surprising and illuminating.

Most clients become very interested and curious about dream analysis and bring in dreams to therapy. The interpretation of a first dream can generally prompt the client into having more dreams. Once the client becomes aware of how relevant much of this seemingly nonsensical material is, he or she will bring in other dreams for analysis. However, clients occasionally report that they do not dream at all. How should a therapist deal with this? Rosenthal stated that some therapists may fall into the trap of the clients' resistance by passively going along with their claim that they do not dream or do not remember their dreams. She states (of the therapist) that "He is like a parent who readily accepts his child's statement: 'I can't just write' or 'clean' or 'read' because it suits the parent not to be bothered" (1978b, p. 229).

What are some common resistances, and how does a therapist deal with the resistant client? The resistance is generally expressed by one or all of these three statements: "I don't dream," "I don't remember my dreams," or "Dreams are not important." How a therapist chooses to deal with these resistances will depend upon the therapist's style and the particular client. However, an understanding of the fear underlying the resistance is important in dealing with it. The therapist may choose to lessen the fear, to attack the fear, or to act in a variety of ways to deal with this fear.

The first resistance, "I don't dream," can be challenged directly and factually with data, since it is a known fact that dreaming is a universal phenomenon. Rosenthal sometimes attacked the narcissism behind the resistance by asking, "Do you think you are different from anybody else in the world?" The client may then admit that he has dreams but that he forgets them. The therapist can then ask, "What do you think a person's intent is when he doesn't remember?" or "Why do you think people forget?" The client may respond that he doesn't know, and the therapist can then say, "He forgets what he doesn't want to remember."

What are some reasons why people may not want to remember their dreams? Clients may or may not be able to relate these spontaneously, but a discussion of some major memory blocks may elicit why clients do not recall their dreams. One block to memory is the client's fear of being exposed to the therapist. Frequently, clients worry about what the therapist will think of them after their unacceptable parts have been seen.

Another common resistance to dream recall is clients' fears of what their unconscious is saying because they are not yet ready to deal with specific issues. Lori, for example, had a very active dream life until a very difficult divorce several years ago. At that point, she had numbed most of her feelings and stopped remembering her dreams. She was afraid that her dreams would evoke feelings that were too painful and that she was not yet ready to confront. Carol was having several vivid and powerful dreams every night after she started attending a dream class. However, she stopped recalling her dreams when her therapist suggested to her that she might be overstimulating herself with them. Carol was also worried that she would have to act right away on some of the conflicts that were appearing in her dreams.

Sometimes people do not recall their dreams because they find the content unacceptable and disown many of the feelings in the dream. It is as though they are saying, "This angry, crazy stuff is not really me." They do not recall their dreams because they feel too embarrassed or afraid of them. Dreams of sexual activity with one's children, parents, and members of the same sex may evoke particular anxiety. Similarly, dreams of violence, blood, deformity, and such physical functions as urinating or defecating can elicit fear or embarrassment.

Other clients may not recall their dreams because they believe it takes a great deal of effort, and they have too many other things they need to do. They see keeping a dream journal and recalling and recording dreams as another chore to add to their busy schedules. In addition, many people feel that they must have at least 8 hours of uninterrupted sleep or they won't be able to function the next day.

Ironically, clients occasionally do not recall their dreams because they are trying too hard, as in the case of Mary, who was putting too much pressure on herself to recall her dreams. Others may tell themselves that they have to remember or the therapist will judge them as inadequate. This pressure to remember may interfere with recall. Similarly, clients may be putting more pressure on themselves by wanting to have a "good," "meaningful," or "interesting" dream and may worry that the therapist will judge them uninteresting or boring if a "good" dream is not produced.

Another common resistance is reflected in a tendency by some clients to put down dreams and minimize their importance. This can generally be dealt with by education and the authoritative providing of information. Hattie Rosenthal might have confronted such a client by asking: "How much do you know about dreams? How much have you read about them? How much thought have you given to dream interpretation?" It is important that this confrontation not be done in a hostile, defensive manner but in a matter-of-fact, authoritative way, with the intent to educate. This confrontation is designed to make the client think rather than to make opinionated statements that are not based on knowledge or reading. Subsequently, the therapist can begin to lecture on dream theory. Clients can be told that they have feelings and thoughts as well as talents and potentials that they might not learn about if it were not for dream analysis. They can also be reassured that the therapist cannot make sense of the client's dreams alone and that a joint effort is required in order to understand dreams. The promise that dream analysis may shorten treatment by reaching core issues earlier can break down resistance, as can the therapist's assurance that clients are not any less acceptable if they show some "unacceptable" impulses. Hattie Rosenthal might have told the patient, "I have a feeling that you may become curious and interested in dreams. It doesn't have to be next time but I think *soon* you will have a dream." In all her years of practice, there was not a single client whom she was unable to stimulate into bringing dreams.

There are other ways to deal with resistances to the importance of dream material. In a seminar that I was teaching on dreams, one of the students, who came from a behaviorally oriented psychology program, rejected dreams because they were not "hard data." Since they could not be observed or measured, she considered them unimportant. I suggested to her to have a dream about her blocks to dreams. She subsequently had a dream where she was going through an underground cave and experienced fears as she explored. Because of this dream, she was able to come to terms with some of her own fears about exploring her unconscious aspects. Sometimes people will have to *experience* the dream before they can declare it meaningful.

In dealing with the resistance of minimizing the importance of dreams, it is important that we appeal to the curiosity and open-mindedness of clients. The clients' fears about exploring unconscious aspects of their personalities can be addressed by reminding them how much of their lives have been spent in school learning about arithmetic, history, geography, and so on, and how little time has been invested in learning about the most important part of their world—themselves. Clients should be reminded that only by learning about themselves and their behavior can they then choose and take responsibility for their actions.

Each fear that underlies a resistance to dream recall can be addressed directly by the therapist and dealt with in a manner comfortable for that particular therapist and client. For example, clients who are worried about what the therapist might think of them if the therapist discovers all of their unacceptable parts can be reassured that they will not be thought less of, and that furthermore, everyone has unacceptable parts. However, these parts need to be recognized in order to make changes in behavior. The therapist can also reassure clients that dream analysis is a team effort, and that the therapist cannot "read" them simply by listening to a dream. It may be that with time, clients can trust themselves to reveal more and more aspects of themselves to the therapist.

Clients who are afraid to look at some of their inner conflicts because they may have to deal with them right away need to be reassured that they have a choice whether they wish to act on the dream message. Just being aware of a conflict doesn't mean they have to make changes immediately. Carla, for example, stopped recalling her dreams when she became aware of some very negative feelings toward her husband. She needed to be reassured that recognition of these feelings did not necessarily mean she had to make any changes in her behavior toward him. It did not mean she had to confront him, get a divorce, or do anything of which she was afraid.

Clients who are afraid to recall their dreams because they find the content unacceptable need to also be reassured that the manifest dream content is different from its latent meaning. Laura, for example, was horrified when she had a dream where she was engaging in sexual activity with her sister. She wondered if that made her "abnormal" or if she had underlying desires for her sister that she did not know about. When we explored the dream further, she realized that it only reflected positive feelings that she was starting to integrate into her perception of her sister. Frequently, the act of making love is symbolic of loving another person and may have little to do with overt sexual feelings. Similarly, dreams about other human functions such as defecation or vomiting may be symbolic of other types of behavior. It is important to reassure the client that these kinds of dreams are very common.

Clients who report that they have little time to devote to their dream life or that the act of recording their dreams can interfere with their functioning the next day can be taught new, creative attitudes about their dream life. Harvey, for example, had a very busy schedule and didn't feel he could do "one more thing." However, from past experience, he also realized the value of dreams and learned to say to himself whenever he felt that it was too much trouble to record his dreams, "I am never too busy if I choose what is most important to my well-being." He also learned to tell himself, "The time I spend working on my dreams will decrease my stress by bringing me inner peace." Harvey also challenged his thinking about needing 8 hours of uninterrupted sleep nightly. He told himself, "I do not need to interrupt my sleep. I will simply remember the first dream upon awakening. However, if a dream is important enough that I awaken from it, working on it may save me many sleepless nights later on." At times he also told himself, "It is creative to have my sleep interrupted with a dream." In addition, clients can be told that they do not need to record each and every dream they have. One dream a week is sufficient to explore in therapy.

Clients who do not appear to have attitudes that may be interfering with dream recall may simply need more specific suggestions for remembering their dreams. The therapist can explore with them in detail the manner in which they are going about trying to recall their dreams. Do they keep a dream journal by the bedside? On the nights that they wish to incubate a dream, do they go to bed with a clear mind? Are they fatigued? Do they write the thoughts of the day and a discussion of the problem on which they wish to work? How do they wake up in the morning? Do they immediately open their eyes? Do they try to go back into the dream state? Do they reject dream fragments right away because they are too short, too unimportant, or because they are only part of a dream? Through careful exploration, the therapist may be able to determine at which stage of dream recall the client is stuck. The therapist can review Gayle Delaney's suggestions for dream recall in detail and reassure clients that if they follow these, they will eventually remember their dreams.

As noted before, clients may occasionally be unable to recall dreams because they are trying too hard and may become anxious about having to produce dreams. In those cases, taking some of the pressure off by stating, "When you are ready, you will have a dream" may be sufficient to decrease the anxiety. The therapist also needs to reassure clients that dreams do not have to be masterpieces, works of art, or interesting on the surface.

Probably the most important factor in recalling dreams is the amount of work clients put into it. It is important to stress to clients the reciprocal nature of the relationship between them and their dreams: They will get from their dreams what they give to them. The therapist should tell clients that if they want to learn something useful about themselves from their dreams, they must have a conscious relationship with their dream life. To have a relationship with one's dreams is to give them the same nurturance one would give a special friend. To develop a meaningful friendship or a meaningful dream life requires the giving of time, attentiveness, and respect. It requires making a commitment to pay attention to this most important aspect of oneself, not only when one wants something from it. It may require getting a special dream journal and making a commitment to write in it regularly. People have reported that when they made a commitment to spend 15 minutes every morning writing *something* in their dream journal, regardless of whether they remembered their dreams or not, they started to recall their dreams. The returns that the dream gives back to the dreamer are manifold.

CONCLUSION

Educating clients about dreams is important in helping them recall and use them to learn about themselves. Clients can learn that every dream is an inner message that has therapeutic implications. The therapist can give clients specific techniques for recalling dreams, which include keeping paper and pencil by the bed before going to sleep, thinking backwards when first awakening, leaving themselves time to record the dream, and not attempting to interpret it before writing it down. The therapist can also give them suggestions for incubating dreams, which include writing down thoughts and feelings of the day and a discussion of the problem to be worked on, along with asking a specific incubation question before going to sleep. The therapist can be aware of common resistances, which are generally expressed in one or all of these statements: "I don't dream," "I don't remember my dreams," or "It doesn't mean anything." The therapist can deal with these common resistances by understanding the fears underlying them. Clients may be fearful of exposing themselves to the therapist, of becoming aware of and dealing with unacceptable or painful issues, or they may be putting too much pressure on themselves to remember. These resistances can be dealt with by education and authoritative providing of information, reassurance about the underlying fears, specific suggestions for dream recall, and the development of creative attitudes for remembering dreams. The therapist can remind clients of the reciprocal nature of the dreamer to his or her dreams and stress that the more time, respect, and energy they give to their dream life, the more they will receive from it.

Chapter 6
The Basic Steps

> *Dreams are the true interpretations of our inclinations, but art is required to sort and understand them.*
>
> Montaigne, *Essays*

Once a client brings in a dream, how does the therapist go about the process of interpretation to get at its meaning? How does the therapist translate from one level of consciousness to another? Dream interpretation consists of interpreting the manifest content into its latent meaning in order to derive a message. It is finding the common denominator between the two levels of consciousness until the dream story can be rewritten. The following dream by a woman in an unhappy marital situation illustrates how this translation between levels can work:

> *I am cold and starved. I go into a restaurant hoping to get some warmth, but it is freezing in there. The server serves three other people before me even though I was there first, and he gives me the leftovers. I am hurt and angry, but I eat the crumbs anyway. I think maybe I should leave but I am afraid that there may not be any other restaurants open. Crumbs are better than nothing. I notice that I am wearing diapers, and I think to myself that if it weren't for the diapers, I would get better service.*

Therapist: "Do you have any feelings as to what this dream is about?"

Client: "No, it all seems so nonsensical. I really can't make any sense out of it."

Therapist: "Can you tell this dream in the third person, as though you are telling a story about someone else?"

Client: "Well, a woman is hungry and cold. She goes to a restaurant to eat, but she doesn't get served, and she only gets the leftovers. She thinks she should leave, but she is afraid she won't find anything else, and besides, crumbs are better than nothing. She is wearing diapers and thinks that if she didn't have these, she might get better service."

Therapist: "What is the general feeling in the dream? How does the dreamer feel?"

Client: "She is cold, hungry, and frustrated. She doesn't get any satisfaction. Others come first, and she only gets the leftovers. She is afraid to leave because there may not be anything better."

Therapist: "Do you see any relationship between those feelings and any that you may be experiencing in your waking life?"

Client: "That sums up pretty accurately how I feel much of the time. I don't feel satisfied in my marriage, everyone else always comes first, and yet I am afraid to leave because there may not be anything else."

Therapist: "Is there anything that interests you most in this dream, anything that is not understandable?"

Client: "Yes, the diapers. What am I doing wearing diapers?"

Therapist: "What is a diaper?"

Client: "A diaper is something that is worn by babies who are helpless and can't care for themselves. Only babies wear diapers."

Therapist: "And what are you reminded of when you think of something you display that is only worn by babies who are helpless and can't take care of themselves?"

Client: "I guess that would be my childish, helpless part that wants to be taken care of. If I stop acting helpless, maybe I will get better service."

Therapist: "Let us look at some of the other elements in the dream. What is a restaurant?"

Client: "A restaurant is a place where you expect to get food and nourishment and warmth."

Therapist: "What are you reminded of in your life when you think of a place where you expect to get nourishment that you are starved for but only get leftovers?"

Client: "My marriage. I am starved for love, affection, and warmth, but I only get the leftovers."

Therapist: "And what is cold?"

Client: "Lack of warmth, like the coldness in our relationship. There is absolutely no warmth in it."

Therapist: "What is a server?"

Client: "A server is someone who provides you with nourishment."

Therapist: "And who would be the person whom you expect to provide you with this warmth and nourishment, who is giving you leftovers instead and putting others ahead of you?"

Client: "My husband."

Therapist: "And who are the three people whom he feeds ahead of you even though you came first?"

Client: "That would probably be his three children, my stepchildren. He always puts them ahead of me, even though I should come first."

Therapist: "And what are crumbs or leftovers?"

Client: "That is what you get after everyone else has eaten. In our house

we usually save that for the dogs, and sometimes it is not even fit for
the dogs. That is what I get from him, attention only when the stepchildren are not there, and most of the time he treats me no better than
you would treat a dog.''

Therapist: ''And why does the dreamer settle for crumbs?''

Client: ''I guess she feels they are better than nothing, and besides, there
may not be any other restaurants. I am afraid to go out on my own
because I may not find anything better.''

Therapist: ''Why don't we retell this dream? You are starving for affection
and warmth but settle for crumbs from your husband, letting him put
his children ahead of you, because you are afraid that you won't find
anything else. You also tell yourself that if you stop acting helpless and
childlike, you may get better treatment from him. What do you think
the message of this dream is for you?''

Client: ''The dream is telling me not to be afraid to ask for what I want
and that if I stop feeling and acting so helpless, I may get him to treat
me better.''

Therapist: ''How can you apply this to your life? Let's look at what the
dreamer can do in the dream so that she can satisfy her needs.''

Client: ''Well, first of all, she can get rid of those diapers if she wants to
be taken seriously. It is ridiculous for a grown woman to be wearing
diapers. Secondly, she can ask for better service. She should tell the
server that she was there first, and she should also let those three people know that she was there first. And if they don't comply, she can
go out until she finds another restaurant. Crumbs are not better than
nothing. They are not at all satisfying.''

Therapist: ''And how can you apply this to your life?''

Client: ''Well, first of all, I should stop telling myself that I am helpless,
and I should not act that way around my husband. Whenever I want
love or attention, I act like a child to get it, either by having a tantrum
or acting so babylike that he has to take care of me. I can also act more
adultlike with the children. I am their stepmother and not someone
who has to compete with them for his attention. I need to let him and
them know that I come first, and that I won't settle for leftovers. And
if he still doesn't give me what I need, then I am going to leave.''

This dream illustrates the translation from one level of consciousness
to another and the rewriting of the dream story into its original story.
There is a constant shifting from one level to another in the interpretation, a constant going back and forth between the dream story and the
story it refers to, between the dreamer in the third person and the client
in the first person. The dream is elaborated on in some detail here to provide a clear example of some of the basic steps in the interpretive process

that will be discussed later in this chapter. In reality, dream interpretation doesn't follow these steps so neatly. The process of interpretation is not always so easy, nor does it always follow a logical series of steps.

Interpreting a dream is very much like doing a jigsaw puzzle. There is no "correct" way to do it. The therapist starts somewhere, and each piece that is fitted in contributes something and makes it easier for the next piece. After a while, all of the pieces fit together. This is how dream analysis is done, slowly and patiently, piece by piece, until the whole can be seen. Sometimes all the pieces are not found, and there is an incomplete puzzle. That is okay. Even if only part of a dream can be interpreted, the client gains something. Maybe the next day, or in a later dream, the missing pieces can be found. It is better to leave a dream incomplete than to put in the wrong pieces and make an incorrect or arbitrary interpretation.

Even though there is no "correct" way to piece the dream puzzle, there are a number of basic steps that can serve as guidelines for the beginning therapist. These steps will be discussed in this chapter and illustrated as they apply to the preceding dream. Before the therapist goes through the basic steps in interpreting a dream it is generally a good idea to ask the client if he or she has any feelings or thoughts about what the dream may be about. This may eliminate many of the steps in the interpretation. Frequently, clients have a pretty good idea about the general meaning of their dreams and will spontaneously bring in associations. Sometimes, as in the dream used in the example, the client will not know to what the dream refers.

The first step in the interpretive process is to *define a pattern*. Every dream, regardless of content, has a theme, a plot in which the dreamer or protoganist is doing something. To get at the dreamer's pattern, it is sometimes helpful to ask the dreamer to repeat the dream in the third person as though it were a story that is happening to another person. This gives the dreamer some distance from the dream and helps him or her see the actions more clearly. Asking specifically about how the dreamer feels or the general mood or feeling in the dream can also illuminate the pattern in the dream. In the preceding example, the therapist's questions ("Can you tell this dream in the third person, as though you are telling a story about someone else?" and "What is the general feeling in the dream? How does the dreamer feel?") help the client and therapist see the pattern in the dream that is being displayed. Once the client summarizes the dreamer's pattern in an impersonal way, as in the preceding example ("She is cold, hungry and frustrated. She doesn't get any satisfaction. Others come first, and she only gets the leftovers. She is afraid to leave because there may not be anything better."), he or she can then deduce from the general to the personal meaning. The therapist prompts her to do this by asking, "Do you see any relationship between those feelings and any that you may be experiencing in your waking life?'' Frequently, clients will report, as this client did, that this pretty accurately summarizes their general condition. From the very first step, defining a pattern, the therapist is shifting from one level of consciousness to another, from one story to another. The common denominator between the two levels of consciousness is the dreamer's pattern, mood, state of being. This basic step of defining the dreamer's pattern gives an idea of what the dream is about.

The second step in interpretation is to *find a focal point* from which to start asking questions. It is generally a good idea to start with that part of the dream that is least understood, the part that is incongruous or doesn't make sense. In the preceding example, the therapist asked the client, ''Is there anything that interests you most in this dream, anything that is not understandable?'' The client replied, ''Yes, the diapers. What am I doing wearing diapers?'' It is not necessary to start with the focal point in doing dream interpretation; however, it is usually helpful, as it is frequently the very incongruity of the focal point that provides the dream message, as in this case—that the dreamer needs to get rid of her childishness in order to have her needs met (''If it weren't for the diapers, I would get better service'').

The third step in dream interpretation is to *define every symbol and get its to-the-point association*. As noted before, a symbol is something that stands for something else and shares with it common characteristics. To arrive at what each symbol stands for, the therapist needs to ask for a definition of the symbol. The words used in the definition and the specific associations to the symbol are the common denominator between the symbol and the object to which it refers. The *to-the-point association* is an association to that particular symbol that provides a link between the dream object and the client's waking life. The symbols in the preceding dream are: ''restaurant, server, other people, leftovers, diapers, cold, starved.'' Let us look at the definitions for each of these symbols and how we arrive from those definitions and associations to the symbol's original meaning:

1. *Symbol*: Diaper
   Definition: ''Something that is worn by babies who are helpless and can't take care of themselves''
   To-the-point association: ''And what are you reminded of when you think of something that you display that is only worn by babies who are helpless and can't take care of themselves?''
   ''I guess that would be my childish, helpless part that wants to be taken care of.''
   Common characteristics: Worn by babies, helpless, can't take care of self.

2. *Symbol*: Restaurant
   Definition: "A place where you expect to get food and nourishment and warmth"
   To-the-point association: "What are you reminded of in your life when you think of a place where you expect to get nourishment and where you are starved for it but only get leftovers?"
   "My marriage."
   Common characteristics: Starved for, expects to get nourishment, only gets leftovers.

3. *Symbol*: Server
   Definition: "Someone who provides you with nourishment"
   To-the-point association: "And who would be the person whom you expect to provide you with warmth and nourishment who is giving you leftovers instead and putting others ahead of you?"
   "My husband."
   Common characteristics: Providing with nourishment, putting others ahead, giving leftovers.

4. *Symbol*: Other people
   Definition: (not asked for)
   To-the-point association: "And who are three people he feeds ahead of you even though you came first?"
   "His three children."
   Common characteristics: Three of them, get served before her even though she should come first.

5. *Symbol*: Crumbs or leftovers
   Definition: "What you get after everyone else has eaten"
   To-the-point association: "In our house we usually save that for dogs, and sometimes it is not even fit for dogs. That is what I get from him, attention only when the stepchildren are not there, and most of the time he treats me no better than you would a dog."
   "They are better than nothing."
   Common characteristics: What you get after everyone else, not fit for a dog sometimes, settles for because she fears there's nothing better.

6. *Symbol*: Cold
   Definition: "Lack of warmth"
   To-the-point associations: "Like our relationship"
   Common characteristics: No warmth.

7. *Symbol*: Starved
   Definition: (not asked for)
   To-the-point association: "I am starved for love, affection and warmth, but I only get the leftovers."
   Common characteristics: Starved for something, doesn't get it, only gets leftovers.

As can be seen from the previous examples, a definition to the symbol and an association to that object provide the link or common denominator between the object and that to which it refers. This process is again a translation from one level to another, and the constant shifting between the dream story and waking life is apparent in the process of interpretation.

Following the translation of all of the symbols, the fourth step in dream interpretation is *rewriting the dream story*. Once all or most of the elements in a dream become clear, the therapist can go through the dream step by step, substituting new meaning to the symbols. This makes the dream story clearer to both therapist and client. In the preceding example, the therapist retells and summarizes the new dream story as follows: "You are starving for affection and warmth but settle for crumbs from your husband, letting him put his children ahead of you, because you are afraid that you won't find anything else. You also tell yourself that if you stop acting helpless and childlike, you may get better treatment from him."

With the retelling of the dream in its new meaning, the therapist helps the client *arrive at the dream message*, which is the fifth basic step in the interpretative process. In the previous example, the therapist asks the client what she thinks the message of the dream is for her, and the client responds, " . . . not to be afraid to ask for what I want and that if I stop acting so helpless, I may get him to treat me better." It is important to have the client verbalize the message, so that it can be acted upon in his or her waking life.

The sixth step in dream interpretation is *applying the dream message to one's life*. In this step, as in the previous ones, there is a shifting from one level of consciousness to another. It is frequently helpful in this step to ask the client to work out a solution *within the dream* and then later apply it to his or her waking life. Most people find it much easier to work out solutions within the dream when there is some distance and objectivity. In the example, the therapist tells the client, "Let's look at what the dreamer can do in the dream so that she can satisfy her needs." The dreamer first finds some solutions within the dream framework, including discarding the diapers, asking for better service, letting them know she was there first, and going to another restaurant if she still continued to receive crumbs. She could then translate this to her waking behavior—that she would stop acting childlike, ask more directly for her needs, become assertive with her family, and leave if the situation didn't change. This last step in dream interpretation, of course, is of essential importance, and much of therapy is devoted to practical application of the dream message.

CONCLUSION

Hattie Rosenthal's method of dream interpretation is one of the few that provides a detailed and clear methodology. The basic steps can serve as guidelines for the beginning therapist and make it easier for him or her to arrive at an interpretation. It is frequently asked if dreams could not be interpreted using a different method and how one can be sure which is the correct interpretation. According to Rosenthal the answer is: "Yes, but if the interpretations are done correctly, all interpretations lead to the same conclusions" (1980, p. 39). Many schools of thought may use entirely different methods to reach the meaning of dreams. Gestalt therapists, for example, may use primarily nonverbal methods to arrive at the same conclusions. However, just as in other forms of psychotherapy, regardless of method or language used, most would hopefully bring the same results and conclusions.

It is important, however, that the therapist interpret a dream based on a theory and method rather than relying on his or her own associations and projections. Rosenthal wrote:

> It is sloven, unscientific and unreliable to use case method without the fundamental concept method. This is like building a house without a solid foundation. A dream analyst who ignores basic theory and merely relies on his imagination and intuition is likely to fail and mislead the total therapeutic process. (1980, p. 39)

It is therefore important to learn dream analysis patiently, step by step, then to do it thoroughly. It is better in the long run to leave a dream uninterpreted than to do one hastily and impulsively. Each of the basic steps in interpretation needs to be learned, and each succeeding chapter will discuss one of these steps in detail. An additional chapter on dream mechanisms is included, as dream mechanisms are part of the dream language and cut across these steps. The last chapter summarizes the process of interpretation.

Chapter 7
Defining a Pattern

Dreams retain the infirmities of our character.
R. W. Emerson, *Demonology*

When a client brings a dream to discuss in therapy, the first thing that a therapist should do is listen very carefully to the dream. As the therapist listens, he or she gets a reaction, a feeling, a first impression and hears a story, a general theme. As the therapist listens to the dream story, he or she tries to get a picture of the *pattern* shown in the story.

What do we mean by a pattern? When the therapist first hears the dream, it frequently sounds nonsensical, even psychotic at times. However, even if it appears rambling and confused, it has a method. Regardless of the dream content, there is always a dreamer, a protagonist. The therapist needs to look at what the dreamer is doing in the dream to define the pattern. This is similar to what a psychologist does when listening to a story told on the Thematic Apperception Test. He or she looks at a general theme or a plot and particularly at what actions, needs, and feelings the dreamer is expressing.

What are some examples of patterns shown in dreams? The protagonist could be engaging in any number of activities, such as comparing him- or herself to others, feeling frustrated in attempts to reach goals, running away from a situation, overreacting to someone, or displaying physical symptoms or engaging in any number of activities. The pattern gives the therapist an idea of the characteristics and dynamics of the client. It is a good diagnostic tool, because it essentially defines the client's defenses, the general manner in which he or she is approaching a problem or situation. As noted in previous chapters, the dream is frequently a reflection of life, and the dreamer's behavior in the dream generally reflects his or her behavior in waking life. While listening to the dream story, the therapist can ask him- or herself, "What is the dreamer doing in this dream? What is his or her pattern?" This helps to weed out the details and focus on the dreamer's actions.

How does a therapist arrive at the pattern? The client tells a dream, and the therapist listens to it. If the therapist tells a client that he or she wants to find out something about him, the client is naturally frightened and may be unable to disclose personal information. The therapist, in appreciating this fear, can ask the client to repeat his or her dream, telling it in the third person, as though it were a true story that happened to someone else. This gives the client some objectivity to the dream and allows him or her to gain a broader perspective on it. For this reason, it is frequently desirable for the therapist to also use the third person when asking questions about the client's actions in the dream. Talking about a "dreamer" can be helpful in giving the client some distance from the problem, so that he or she can look at some solutions. Frequently, clients are able to see solutions to long-standing problems within their dreams that they would be unable to arrive at in their waking lives. In the dream discussed in the previous chapter, for example, the woman was able to arrive at several appropriate, alternative ways of dealing with the dilemma within the dream and later apply these solutions to her life.

Having the client recount the dream in the third person has another advantage, since it allows the therapist to hear the dream for the second time and to clarify the pattern in his or her mind. The client should be asked to briefly repeat the dream in the third person, without too many superfluous details, simply to summarize the basic actions. To attain further clarification of the pattern, the client can be asked, "What is your general impression?" or "What is the dreamer doing?" Sometimes, the therapist can ask about the general mood or feeling in the dream to arrive at the dreamer's pattern. For example, after recounting a long, detailed narrative, the dreamer may summarize the general feelings in the dream as those of frustration, as in the following statement: "The dreamer keeps wanting to get somewhere, but other people get in his way, and he can never get what he wants." Or the client may summarize a long, detailed dream by saying, "The general mood is that of nostalgia. The dreamer is reminiscing about the past and feels both happy and sad about it."

Once the general theme or pattern of a dream is elicited, the therapist can ask whether the client sees any relationship between that general pattern and him- or herself. At this point, the client can relate the actions of the dreams to his or her waking life. This is the "confession," so to speak. As a rule, it is easier to arrive at a general theme and then to deduce from the general or impersonal to the personal meaning. Frequently, people see the similarities between their actions in their dreaming and waking lives immediately and will make comments to that effect.

The following example depicts how the actions in dreams summarize the basic actions in reality. Joan, a woman who was working in therapy on her eating problems, was asked to have a dream about the role that food played in her life. She recounted the following dream:

All the people in my house—my husband and my daughters—are in the livng room doing something. I am in a corner of the house, off to the side, and my project is to put these rectangular food shapes, one on top of the other, so that they fit exactly.

Joan's dream succinctly encapsulated the essence of her dilemma. Her pattern was to be off to the side, engaging in some meaningless food activity, while the rest of her family were in the mainstream of life.

John's dream about his marital situation also summarized his problems succinctly. In his dream, John was looking at three people standing in a triangle and thinking that it was a mess. It was fairly easy to generalize from the dream to this own personal situation, where he was looking at the mess from his relationships with his wife and another woman.

Although the dreamer's pattern is fairly clear in most dreams, sometimes there may be some difficulty in arriving at it. A helpful exercise is to take out all of the nouns in the dream and to replace them with indefinite articles to get at the basic theme, pattern, or story line. If the therapist substitutes the words *someone* or *something* for every noun in the dream story, the pattern becomes much clearer. Let us take the following dream as an example:

I am at a picnic and sitting there with Tom. We are drinking beer and I am looking for ice to cool his beer bottle, but I can't seem to find any. I want to cool his beer so that I can go running and then eat my sandwich. Before I can eat it, however, I see John and Dick who need my help. I go to help them, and then the next thing I see is that my grandmother has packed away my sandwich, and I never get to eat it.

Rewriting the dream with indefinite articles may result in the following version:

I am somewhere with someone. I am trying to do something for him before I can go do something I want. Before I can get at something I want, however, I have to help others. When I come back, someone has put away what I want, and I stay hungry.

When we weed out the nouns, the story becomes much clearer, and it is easier to get at the dreamer's pattern. The above pattern may be summarized as follows: ''The dreamer doesn't do what she wants until she takes care of others first. By then, it is too late for her to meet her needs, and she feels frustrated.'' Following that, the therapist can ask the client if she sees any relationship between the dreamer's actions and her own. For example, does she always put others first and end up feeling frustrated? Later inquiry would focus on the specific symbols in the dream. However, for the time being, the client's pattern in her dream summarizes her basic conflict or dilemma quite accurately. Although the specific content may vary from dream to dream, frequently the basic style or pattern of the dreamer remains the same.

As an exercise, several dreams are presented here so that the reader can have some practice in defining a pattern in a dream. For this to be most helpful, the reader should attempt to define the basic pattern in each of the dreams before reading further. The following dream was told by a middle-aged woman:

> I am going out to either take out the garbage or bring in the paper. I know there were men outside doing construction work. I know I have no clothes on but I go out anyway. One man said, "She has a short robe on." The other nodded in agreement, even though they both knew I didn't. I go along with the pretense and tug at my imaginary robe.

The first step is to let the dreamer generalize the dream content in an impersonal way and then deduce from the general to the personal meaning. This dreamer said, "The protagonist is doing something unconventional, and it's okay. She is exposing herself and people can see her for what she is, and both she and others are comfortable with it." To get to the personal meaning, she was asked, "Do you see anything of yourself in this dream?" She recounted that the prior week she had bought some furniture because she liked having company and was embarrassed of her "bare" room. However, the furniture was "just not her," and she had returned it. The dream message was in essence confirming what she had known unconsciously: "Be comfortable, be yourself; if you can accept yourself as you are and be comfortable, so can others."

The following dream was also related by the same woman:

> I had taken the long tapers out of the refrigerator to use for Len's birthday, and I noticed that the bottoms had gotten stubby. I said, "That's okay. I will just use a different holder."

In this dream, just as in the previous one, the dreamer is not very concerned with appearances. Once the basic pattern is elicited, then she can be asked how this applies to her current life situation. In this case, as in the previous one, her dream reflected her actions in her waking life. The dreamer used to be concerned about doing everything just right for Len, someone she cared for deeply. In her dream as well as in reality, she was able to become more casual about appearances with him.

The following dream was related by a man who was encountering frustration in his life:

> I am trying to get into a store, and it is locked. I just don't know what to do. Then somehow Mike is with me, and he reminds me that I have the key, that in fact I've always had the key that can unlock this door and any other door.

The dreamer is frustrated but then is reminded that he has the key to solve his problem and that he has always had it. The dream message in this case was that he had within himself the solution to his frustrations. Further analysis of the dream would clarify what the solution was.

Here is another dream told by a professional woman:

Several of my friends are going to the movies to see "Black Sunday." We get chil-
dren's tickets, trying to sneak in and go at a cheaper rate. I try to sneak by the lady
who takes the tickets, and I guess she is running after me as if to hit me for sneaking
in. In the moviehouse I see some co-workers and their spouses. They are dressed in
tuxedos, and I hope that they don't see me.

The basic pattern in this dream is that the dreamer is trying to pass as a
child and is afraid she will be punished for it. She is also worried that
others will see her childishness. Further inquiry in this dream can focus
on the specific details, for example, the name of the movie, the ticket lady,
and so on.

Here are more dreams, which have been condensed for the purpose of
instruction:

I am on a highway. I am trying to get to Tollison but I can't seem to get there. There
is a canal in the way, and there is a highway with lots of fast cars.

The main theme is that the dreamer is trying to get somewhere but is
blocked. Further analysis would focus on where he wants to go and what
is blocking him.

The following dream also involves driving a vehicle:

I am driving in my car, going up 48th Street. The brakes don't seem to be working.
I try to stop at a stop sign but the car just slows down and I coast and cross the
street. There is a woman with me in the car. I am worried about what she thinks
of me, and I'm surprised that she is unconcerned and nothing happened.

The dreamer cannot seem to "slow down." Her brakes (controls) are not
working, and she is concerned about how she is seen by others.

Here is another dream involving a car:

I am trying to get to Prescott, but my car is not working. I stand on the side of the
road, thinking I will be safe, but I get hit anyway. My husband is with me.

The dreamer thinks that if she stands to the side, she is immune to
tragedy. She finds out she is not. This woman had been avoiding the problem of communicating with her husband, thinking that if she avoided the
problem, she would be safe. Her unconscious told her otherwise.

The following dream was told by a woman whose life was going
smoothly:

I am in a house with a father, son and daughter. I know how the story is going to
end. My brother, John, is in it too. At the end, when I am supposed to kill someone
(according to the book or story or whatever), it doesn't end that way. The person
kisses me instead, and it ends on a very positive note.

The basic pattern in this dream is that the story does not go according to
the script but ends on a positive note instead. This was essentially a

parallel of this dreamer's life, in that the tragedy she expected to continue from an unhappy childhood involving her father and brother never happened, and her life had a happy ending instead.

The following dream was told by a middle-aged man who was depressed:

> *I had a dream about a play that I was watching, and in this play there was a man committing suicide. That's about all I remember in the dream. I recall thinking that this is a stupid thing to do.*

In the dream, the dreamer is looking at suicide as an option and rejecting it. The basic pattern in this dream may be more difficult to define than in the previous examples because the protagonist is not the dreamer. Most of the action in the dream focuses on the actor. The therapist can define the dreamer's pattern by focusing on what the *dreamer* is doing in the dream; in this case, observing someone killing himself and thinking that is a stupid thing to do. Frequently, clients will bring in dreams where the focus appears to be on another person. The therapist should not lose track of the fact that this is the *client's* dream and ask, "What is the *dreamer* doing in this dream?" or "Why is the *dreamer* having a dream about X?" When the main focus of a dream is on a person other than the dreamer, it is most likely a means of distancing oneself from the issue or problem, as though it belongs to someone else.

In the following dream, the protagonist is an animal, not a person:

> *This is a dream about a pig who is doing tricks. I think that the pig has to do these tricks in order not to get abused, in order to protect himself.*

As in the previous dream, the dreamer is looking at the behavior of someone else and wondering about that behavior for himself. The basic pattern here is that the dreamer thinks that sometimes one has to do tricks in order not to get abused and to protect oneself. To get at the personal meaning of this dream, the dreamer was asked if there was a relationship between this pattern and his current life. The dreamer related this to his work situation, in that sometimes he had to play the game in order to protect himself.

The following dream is another example where much of the action is centered on another character:

> *I am standing by the door to Jane's office, and Jane is very loud and boisterous. Someone asks her a question, and she really yells at the top of her voice. It is so loud. She sounds so aggressive.*

As in the previous dreams, the dreamer draws attention away from herself by focusing on another person's behavior. In this dream, the dreamer is observing another person's aggressive behavior. Although she doesn't state what she is doing and focuses on another character, she is concerned about being too aggressive. To get at the dreamer's pattern, the therapist might ask her what she is doing in the dream and what her reactions are to Jane's behavior. The dreamer may be uncomfortable with loud, aggressive behavior and concerned about being aggressive herself.

Clients will frequently bring in long, rambling dreams that may leave the therapist confused about the central action. These dreams are more difficult; however, even with these, a summary of the dreamer's basic actions provides the pattern of the dreamer, as in the following example:

> There are many parts to this dream. I somehow have a bomb in my hand which I need to dispose of, and I am walking on this metal railing which is very tight and which goes up and down, and I hold this bomb very carefully, afraid that it will fall off. There are a few other people walking with me—I am not sure who they are— and one of them says something to me. I am trying to pay attention to him, and then we are in a restaurant or something like that, and there are two tables there, and on one table there are three people, I think, a man, a woman, and a child. I think there is a family sitting at the other table as well, also three people, I think. I sense that they want me to talk to them, but somehow I realize that I should not interfere. I think I am still holding the bomb, and I keep worrying that it will go off. There is another scene after that. I have a sense that I am walking with some child, but I don't remember all of the details. Then I also remember a dog. I think I was in some kind of a store, and there are groceries and canned goods on the shelves, and the dog is being very ferocious. I think it is an Irish setter or something like that. It goes all over the shelves, and it knocks down the cans, and there is no controlling it. I am not sure what happens next, but somehow I am on the streets again, and then I am going down an orange stairway. I think I get rid of the bomb, but I am not sure. It is a long, confusing dream, and there are other parts to it. I don't really recall all of them.

Although this dream is long, it does in fact have a central theme and is less confusing than some other dreams. To get at the general theme, the therapist can try to tune out the details and focus on the main action, in this case, that the dreamer is carrying something dangerous and is trying to dispose of it. Along the way, there are people with whom she decides not to interfere and a dog that is ferocious. The general pattern here is of the dreamer trying to dispose of a bomb. To get at this, the therapist can ask the client, "What is the general feeling in the dream?" "What is the dreamer doing?" After eliciting the general pattern of the dreamer, the therapist can then ask if there is any similarity between it and the dreamer's waking life.

CONCLUSION

The first step in dream interpretation is to define the dreamer's pattern. The therapist does this by listening intently to the dream and getting a reaction to it. Regardless of the length and the content of the dream, there is always a dreamer engaging in some activity. In attempting to define the dreamer's pattern, the therapist can ask him- or herself while listening to the dream: "What is the dreamer doing in the dream?" To get at the pattern, the therapist can ask the client to discuss the dream content in a general manner and from there to arrive at the personal meaning. The therapist can also do this by asking the client to repeat the dream in the third person, as if it were a story he or she has heard. The client can be asked about the general mood and feeling displayed in the dream. Following this, the therapist can ask if there is a similarity between the dream mood and actions and the client's conscious frame of mind. Once the similarities between the dream and waking life are made, further inquiry can focus on the other dream details. The next chapters will review the remaining steps in dream interpretation.

Chapter 8
The Focal Point

Why does the eye see a thing more clearly in dreams
than the imagination when awake?
Leonardo da Vinci, *The Notebooks of*
Leonardo da Vinci

Once the dream pattern is defined, where does the dream inquiry begin? There are usually so many details that a therapist may not know where to start. In interpreting a dream, a therapist can really start anywhere, then connect the different parts to obtain a gestalt, a totality of the parts. It is usually helpful to look for a focal point, a point from which to start interpretation and view all the other parts.

What should be chosen as the focal point in the dream? The therapist should choose that part that is *least understandable*, the most vague, the most mysterious, the part that does not fit. Sometimes the focal point is obvious and can immediately be recognized. At other times, it is not so easy to spot. In those cases, the therapist can go to the next step until the focal point becomes recognizable. Frequently, however, the focal point can be used as a starting point, and many times it provides the key to the dream meaning.

In looking for a focal point, the therapist can ask: "What is inconsistent with the rest of the dream? What does not fit? What is not understandable? What is out of context? What is not congruent?"

Here are some examples of dreams that have focal points that are easily recognizable.

> *I am standing in line in a cafeteria, together with three of my friends. John gets some roast beef, Jerry gets steak, and Jim gets veal. They pay for their meals. On my plate there is a four leaf clover. I don't have to pay for it.*

The focal point in this dream is fairly easy to recognize. The four leaf clover is clearly out of context. On hearing this dream, the most obvious question is "What is a four leaf clover doing in a cafeteria?" What the four leaf clover stands for, however, may provide the key to the rest of the dream.

86

In this particular case, the four leaf clover represented good luck to the dreamer. The dream reflected to him that everyone else had to work hard for his nourishment, but he could get his through luck.

In the following dream, the focal point also provides the key to the meaning of the dream:

> My father was coming to visit, and I was anxious to please him. It was hot, and I wished we had a pool. Then suddenly this fiberglass piece—a pool-spa—arrived, and we were able to swim.

The focal point was the fiberglass piece; the dreamer stated that "no such thing exists." The dream was a reminder to her that pleasing her father was an impossibility and that there was nothing she could do to change that. Her father had originally wanted a son and had several daughters instead.

A few more dreams will be recounted here for purposes of instruction. The reader can attempt to pick out the focal point in each dream after reading it before going further. The following dream was told by a woman in her forties:

> I am at the gynecologist's office. I have cancer, and he is testing me for it. He has to insert a ball through my vagina, and I have to lie very still and be very relaxed so that the ball can go through. I use hypnosis to relax and am able to do it. I recall that the name of my treatment is photosynthesis.

What doesn't fit here? Although there are many elements that stand out in this dream, e.g., the ball, cancer, hypnosis, they are all internally consistent. Photosynthesis is clearly out of context and is again the key to understanding this dream. In this case, the dreamer defined it as "converting negative energy into positive growth".

The following dream was told by a recently married woman:

> I am in a store, and I am looking all over to find matching pants for John and me for our wedding. I look all over and can't seem to find them. Then suddenly, I look in the store windows, and I find some other things I like.

What is inconsistent or incongruent here? The therapist's first reaction is, "Since when does a bride wear pants to a wedding?" The matching pants in this dream serves as a focal point and provides the key to interpreting this dream. The dreamer in this case had been concerned about "who wears the pants" in the family. She was searching for a relationship of equality but could not find it. In the dream, the matching pants also pointed out to her that in her search for an equal relationship, she had inappropriately suppressed some of her "feminine," nurturant, affectionate feelings.

A woman related this dream after several weeks of psychotherapy:

I am in a barber shop. I am angry at waiting for the barber to come and cut my hair. There is a young kid smoking. I speak up and tell him not to. He stops and then starts again. I tell him again to stop.

The part that is incongruous here is the barber shop, as women do not go to barbers. This detail was very important in the dream, since the client's major issue in psychotherapy was accepting her homosexual orientation. Her dream reflected her acceptance in her waking life. As she related, "I am now cleaning up my act and getting rid of the clutter." The dream also reflected her assertiveness and speaking up.

The following dream was told by a man in his late thirties:

I am preparing a homework assignment for a history course. I am on a bicycle, and I have to drop my child off before the course. I am supposed to make a presentation to the class, together with another person. He tells me he'll talk about "The Kings of War." I do not remember that it was his assignment. Mine is vague. I'm not clear about what I read in the book. The scene shifts. I drop my child off at the baby-sitter's. At first I don't remember where to take him and it's getting dark. Then I remember where to take him, and I take him there. Then the scene shifts to a parking lot cafeteria. Others are eating, and I eat a bit of their foods. These people are actors. My class is presenting a paper at this time, and there's another class at this time. It's not time for me to give my presentation so I want to go to the other class, but I want to hear the students' presentation. It would help me, for the test. People are clowning around and eating. I don't get my own food but I get food from them. They are eating strange food.

What is the pattern here? What is the focal point? The general impression in this dream is of the dreamer's unpreparedness and indecisiveness. The "Kings of War" is out of context and clearly a contrast to the rest of the dream. It can be used as a point of inception.

Many times a specific title or phrase can be used as a focal point, as in the previous dream. The dreamer has gone to great lengths to dream about and mention this phrase, and it is no coincidence that it appears there. In the dream discussed prior to this one, the word *photosynthesis* was the focal point of the dream. In that dream as well, a name or title stood out in contrast to the rest of the dream.

Frequently, the focal point focuses attention directly on the client's neurotic or self-defeating behavior, as in the following dream:

I am in a car on the street leading to our house. I am in the back driving, and there are other people in the car. Helen is in the front seat. I ask her to turn on the lights. She tries to but can't seem to. She pushes the wrong button or something. The car goes faster and gets out of control, nearly hitting a pedestrian. I wake up.

The unexplained part here is that the dreamer is driving the car from the back seat. In this case, the focal point calls attention directly to the dreamer's self-defeating actions.

The following dream was recounted by a clinical psychologist:

I am working as a dentist but I know very little about it and have never done any-one's teeth. This man comes to have his teeth cleaned and tonsils removed. I go to my boss and tell him I have no experience taking out tonsils. How do you do it? He tells me it's very simple and elementary. I feel bad I have shown him how ignorant I am but then I shrug. I clean up this guy's teeth. He is a young, good-looking man, and I find him attractive. I tell him his teeth are really nice. I remem-ber seeing just gums, unlike my cavities, and I comment on how nice they are. The guy is a dentist himself and wants to watch me take out his tonsils. I think I do that.

The immediate question that comes to mind is, ''What is a clinical psychol-ogist doing cleaning teeth?'' The absurdity of this highlights the dreamer's unconscious notion that she should be able to do everything. This quick-ly gets to the root of the problem: the dreamer's perfectionism.

Often, the focal point is what is hidden in a dream or what the dreamer is not saying. The focal point can be what is either omitted or not called attention to. For example, John had this dream:

I am standing in a house that has a basement and three stories in it. The basement is dark and dim, and I explore it from bottom to top. I think the first floor is where my mother and father lived, and the third floor has my brothers in it. That is all I remember in this dream.

The focal point is the second floor, which is omitted in the dream. The therapist is naturally curious about that and may wish to start the inquiry with this detail.

The following dream is also significant in what it omits:

I am wearing some kind of a ski outfit or snowsuit. Although I know I don't look perfect, I am very pleased with myself, and I feel very good about the way I look. I have a white cane in my hand, the kind that is used by blind people. I am also wearing a ski mask, with holes for the eyes and nose. I realize that I don't have a face underneath the mask. I remember thinking that I have three handicaps, but I don't know what those are.

The dreamer in this case could clearly define two handicaps: her blindness symbolized by the white cane (she had recently been informed prior to this dream that she might lose her vision) and her depression, which was sym-bolized by her facelessness. The focal point in the dream is the third handicap.

Sometimes the focal point of a dream can be an unusual or inconsis-tent feature, as in the following dream told by a young man who had a series of unsuccessful relationships in the past and was now contemplat-ing marriage. He had come to therapy primarily to find out about the rea-sons for his unsatisfactory relationships. He related this dream:

I think that I am about to marry Marion, but before I can get married, I have to go through some kind of pre-wedding ceremony. I have to go around ten fires that are very beautiful and intense, but what is unusual about these fires is that they do not give off any heat, that somehow all the heat goes inside, and then they burn off very quickly. I am just fascinated by these fires.

What is most interesting about this dream is that the fires are not giving off any heat. These fires described the dreamer's previous relationships, which were with beautiful women who fascinated him. Like his relationships, the fires were intense at first but quickly burned out. He recognized that he was choosing beautiful, narcissistic women who were not giving him any warmth and who were only capable of loving themselves. The focal point in this dream is the fires that the young man needed to look at before he engaged in another "hot" relationship.

In the following dream, as in the preceding one, an unusual feature also serves as the focal point:

> Bill and I bought a new trailer, the kind we had always wanted to buy when we retired, a kind of recreational vehicle. In the dream, I am going through every room in that trailer, and I am looking at the furniture there. The living room area has blue furniture, my favorite color, and it has a dinette and a couch and all the things you find in trailers. There is also a bath and toilet area which seems just right for us. Our bedroom has a bed and a dresser. The bed is very pretty, but it only has three legs, and I wonder if it can support us. Then my kids come in and look at it too.

The bed's three legs serve as the focal point in the dream. This detail is highlighted for good reason. The dream reflected and emphasized some of the dreamer's misgivings about living the rest of her life with her husband. She recognized that something was missing in their sexual relationship and wondered if their marriage could be sustained.

The focal point is more difficult to spot in the following dream:

> I had a dream about Judy. I don't know why I should be dreaming about her. In the dream, she is upset with her co-workers about something—I think she thought that she was working harder than any of them or that it was unfair or something to that effect. Anyway, she was yelling and crying, overreacting to the whole situation instead of talking it over with them. This is so typical of what Judy always does.

The focal point here is the dreamer, precisely because she is not mentioned. All of the attention is on Judy. What is not noted is the dreamer's reaction to Judy's behavior. Does she see anything of herself in Judy? Why is she dreaming about Judy at this time? What message is she telling herself?

CONCLUSION

The preceding dreams have provided examples of focal points that can be used to start the dream inquiry after arriving at the dreamer's pattern. To get to the focal point, it is frequently helpful to ask the client, "What interests you most in this dream?" or "What stands out most for you?" Sometimes the client can be asked, "Is there anything in this dream that doesn't make sense?" or "What doesn't fit here?" Usually the client can relate the part of the dream that he or she finds most puzzling or intriguing. Sometimes, the therapist may suggest a focal point if the client cannot come up with an answer alone. For example, in the "Kings of War" dream discussed at the beginning of the chapter, after getting a general impression of the dream, the therapist might say, "Everything is vague and confused in this dream. Is there anything that makes a definite statement? Is there anything that is a contrast in this dream?" Or the therapist can call attention to the focal point directly and ask the client to explain it. For example, in the dream where the dreamer is driving from the back seat, the therapist may ask right away why the dreamer is driving from the back instead of the front seat.

Although the therapist can usually find a point to focus on to start the dream inquiry, occasionally this may be difficult. That is not important. As noted before, a therapist can start the analysis anywhere and then attempt to fit the pieces together to interpret the dream. If a focal point from which to start the dream interpretation process can not be found, the therapist can go on to defining each symbol in the dream and getting the dreamer's associations to it.

Chapter 9
Definitions and
to-the-Point Associations

The mind asleep hath clear vision.
Aeschylus, *Eumenides*

A dream consists of symbols that are unique to the individual. In order to arrive at the symbol's meaning, the client has to *define* it. Otherwise, this can create some confusion between the therapist and the client. To illustrate, let us assume that a dreamer had a dream that he was watching a movie. What does "movie" mean? We can ask several people to define the word, and we will get several definitions. For example, one person might say, "A movie is a place where you sit in the dark and hold hands with someone." Another might say, "A movie is something that people watch when they are bored and want to be entertained." A third person could reply, "A movie is something that shows a representation of something else." Even though at first glance, the definition of a word may seem obvious, several people will define the same term differently. Therefore, the therapist should never assume a definition but should ask the client directly for it.

When asking someone to define a word, it is important to ask, for example, "What is a movie?" rather than "What is a movie to you?" The first question will elicit a definition of the word; the second may result in numerous associations that can take the therapist further and further away from the symbol. The method of arriving at a symbol's meaning through defining it is very similar to Gayle Delaney's dream interviewing method (1979). Delaney asks the dreamer to define and describe the object to her as though she were someone from another planet who has never heard of it and does not know what it is. The method makes a great deal of sense, since symbols and the objects they stand for share common characteristics. The common characteristics are usually inherent in the definition of the object. For example, a bomb can be defined as "something extremely dangerous and explosive unless you hold it carefully and only dispose of it in the right places and at the right times." The same characteristics in the definition could also describe a person's violence. Every symbol has a common denominator with the object it represents and shares common characteristics with it.

To translate the symbol into its original meaning, the therapist asks for a definition of the symbol and a *to-the-point* association to it. The to-the-point association is directly related to the content of the dream, as opposed to *free associations*, which may hide and detract from the issue. In Freud's method of free association, the patient associates freely to an object and continues to associate to each succeeding association. Rosenthal recommended associating *directly* to the object, and it is for this reason that she labeled these associations to-the-point. Let us get back to the symbol of a bomb. In free associating to that symbol, the client may say something like this: "bomb . . . tomb . . . grave . . . cemetery . . . I buried my dog last week . . . I was feeling morose that day . . . I lost my sweater then . . . we had a history exam . . . " etc. These free associations may detract from the issue and allow the dreamer to get away from the specific content of the dream. With to-the-point associations, on the other hand, the client, after defining a bomb as "something extremely dangerous and explosive unless you hold it carefully and only dispose of it in the right places and at the right times," could give his or her own specific associations to the bomb, e.g., "I don't like bombs. I used to work as a demolition expert, but I couldn't handle it and nearly got killed a couple of times. I have decided since then not to have anything to do with bombs and haven't been near them for the past five years." The to-the-point association is frequently a memory of the object and the dreamer's particular experiences with it. To get to-the-point associations, the therapist can ask the client, "What part has a bomb played in your life?" Frequently, the dreamer will spontaneously associate to the symbol, for example, "I used to work as a demolition expert," and so forth.

The combination of the definition to the symbol and its to-the-point association is one of the most effective ways of arriving at the symbol's meaning. The definition is the conscious, objective association to the symbol, whereas the to-the-point association is the spontaneous, subjective association. Combining the characteristics of the symbol derived from both these methods and asking the client what else in his or her life is reminiscent of the same characteristics usually results in understanding the symbol's underlying meaning.* In the preceding example, the client could

---

*This is similar to the concepts of "explanation" and "association" used by Jung to gain a more precise reading of the dreamer's reaction to the symbols. Through "explanation" of the symbols, the dreamer essentially defines their characteristics; through "association," the client provides his or her own experiences and memories to these symbols. The combination of explanation and association provides a more accurate indicator of what the symbol means to the dreamer (Greene, 1979).

be asked, ''What are you reminded of in your life right now when you think of something that is dangerous and explosive unless you hold it carefully and dispose of it in the right places and times, which you don't like, that has nearly killed you a few times and that you have not had anything to do with for years?'' The client might then state, ''My violent temper.''

The to-the-point associations are not only to the symbol but to the definition of the symbol. For example, a person dreaming of a jack-o-lantern, who defines it as ''a vegetable that is round, has a hard outside but a hollow inside, and is used only infrequently'' could be asked, ''What else is like a vegetable that is round, has a hard outside but is hollow inside and used only infrequently?'' The client might immediately respond, ''My brain—I was just thinking the other day, I feel like a vegetable sometimes, and I haven't been using it. Most of the time it feels empty.'' When getting a definition to an object, the therapist can ask, ''In what or where else do you see the same qualities or characteristics?'' The symbol and the words describing it frequently trigger a specific association and lead to the accurate meaning of the symbol.

A few more examples will be provided to illustrate how to arrive at a symbol's meaning through its definition and to-the-point association, since this is one of the most difficult steps in dream interpretation and one where many clinicians first get stuck. Mark recounted the following dream:

> I dreamed that there was a lion that was threatening to come into the bed where my wife and I were sleeping.

Therapist: ''Define lion.''
Client: ''A lion is an animal that is ferocious, out of control, and needs to be restrained.''
Therapist: ''What part has a lion played in your life?''
Client: ''I don't like lions, I am terrified of them and only see them occasionally. In fact, when I go to the zoo, I avoid the lions' cages.''
Therapist: ''What are you reminded of when you think of something that is ferocious, out of control, that you are terrified of, avoid at all costs, and only let out occasionally, that is threatening to come into your and your wife's bed?''
Client: ''My anger.''

Let us look at another dream to see how the combination of defining the symbol and giving a to-the-point association or specific memory to it elucidates what it may stand for. Cathy related the following dream:

> I dreamed that I was giving birth to six babies, and they just kept coming, one after the other, becoming chickens as they came out. One of the babies has something wrong with her left foot, but my husband is with me, and he tells me that we can handle it.

Therapist: "What are babies?"

Client: "Babies are something new that you give birth to which grow up to be something wonderful. I like them."

Therapist: "What are chickens?"

Client: "Chickens are also something new and young that grow up. These chickens looked just like the chickens that my artist friend draws. They are fragile and beautiful. Her drawings are very creative and artistic."

Therapist: "What six things in your life are you giving birth to that are new, beautiful, fragile, creative and artistic and which can grow into something wonderful?"

Client: "My practice, my work with children, my starting a new program, my art work, my working at _____, and my going to _____ to get some training."

Therapist: "What is wrong with the left foot?"

Client: "The left foot is twisted, just like my daughter's was last month after she had the accident. It is a deformity, a handicap, but it was a minor hurdle and we overcame that."

Therapist: "What comes to your mind involving your new creations when you think of a deformity or handicap that is really only a minor hurdle which you can overcome?"

Client: "That any problems I am having are really only minor ones, and that I can deal with them."

In this dream, the client's own specific associations to the chickens and the twisted left foot provided clues to the meanings of the symbols. This dream again illustrates the individuality of symbols and that therapists can only get at their meaning through the client's own particular experiences with those symbols.

Symbols are unique to the dreamer and depict the dreamer's own memories with them. Linda, for example, had a dream about a gun hidden in a loaf of Italian bread.

Therapist: "What is a gun?"

Client: "It is a weapon that is dangerous and deadly. I hate guns."

Therapist: "What is bread?"

Client: "Bread is something you eat; it is basic nourishment."

Therapist: "And what are you reminded of when you think of something dangerous underneath the guise of nourishment and that is Italian in origin?"

Client: "My family!"

Linda was of Italian origin, and this image very accurately and picturesquely summarized her family interactions. The combination of the defi-

nitions of the symbols and their to-the-point associations will usually elicit
the meaning of those symbols.

In the following dream, which was already discussed in a previous chapter, the symbol is again unique to the dreamer, and its meaning is arrived
at through the combination of a definition and to-the-point association:

> *I observe a pig who is doing tricks. I think he has to do these tricks in order not
> to get abused, to protect himself.*

Therapist: "What is a pig?"
Client: "A pig is an animal who looks dumb but is really quite smart."
Therapist: "What part has a pig played in your life?"
Client: "I grew up on a pig farm! That was my livelihood."
Therapist: "What comes to your mind in relation to your livelihood when
you think of playing tricks in order to protect yourself, or of looking
dumb but actually being quite smart underneath?"
Client: "That describes me in my work situation exactly. Sometimes you
have to look like you don't know what is going on for your own protec-
tion."

In the following dream, paying attention to the specific characteristics
of the symbol clarifies what the dream is about:

> *I am driving down a road, and it suddenly becomes very dark. I become terrified be-
> cause someone gets into the car with me and grabs my chest.*

Therapist: "What comes to your mind when you think of feeling terrified,
in the dark, and that has to do with the chest?"
Client: "My wife's cancer, of course."

This man's wife had a mastectomy recently, and her breast cancer was
a terrifying intrusion into their lives. The very words in the dream are used
to trigger an association to the symbol in this case.

Frequently, we use other people as symbols for different aspects of ourselves. By defining and describing these people, the client can see which
aspects of him- or herself these individuals may represent. Many times
the persons dreamed about could also represent themselves, particularly if they are individuals close to the dreamer, for example, spouses. In
other cases, they could stand for a group of people. For example, John
could stand for "my boss" and bosses in general; Jane could stand for
"my co-worker" and co-workers as a group. In many cases, however,
people in our dreams refer to different aspects of ourselves, particularly
when these figures are people we don't know or rarely see. Frequently,
these individuals are famous personalities, and the dreamer identifies with
certain aspects of them. Again, it is necessary to have the client's (and
not the therapist's) association to that particular person by asking him or
her to describe the person's characteristics, as in the following example:

Client: "I dreamed that I was embracing Elke Sommers."

Therapist: "Who is Elke Sommers?"

Client: "She is a movie star."

Therapist: "Tell me about her."

Client: "She is someone who left her husband, an older man, and she is now making it on her own. She is also very artistic."

Therapist: "Do you see any aspects of her in yourself?"

Client: "I left my husband, an older man, as well, and now I am making it on my own. I am also quite artistic. I guess she would symbolize the artistic part of me that is making it on my own."

In the following dream, a movie star is also used as a symbol:

> *I am somewhere, and Richard Burton takes me for lunch. I don't know where we are going or how long we will be there, but I just drift along. The car is going fast, and I know I should put on the brakes, but I wonder what he will think of me if I do.*

Therapist: "Who is Richard Burton?"

Client: "He is a movie star."

Therapist: "Tell me about him."

Client: "Well, he is someone who has gotten married many times. His relationships never last. That's about all I can think of."

Therapist: "Do you see any aspects of that in yourself?"

Client: "He reminds me of all of the men I go out with. My relationships never last long either. I go from one person to another."

In a dream in which different characters are involved, the client is frequently unaware of which aspects of him- or herself these figures may represent until he or she starts to talk about them, as in the following example:

> *I dreamed that I saw my brother-in-law whom I hadn't seen in ages. I was so happy to see him. I didn't know how much I had missed him. Then he somehow turned into my Uncle Ed.*

Therapist: "Tell me about your brother-in-law."

Client: "My brother-in-law is a fine man. I haven't seen him in years, and I really miss him very much. I don't know when or if I will see him again. But I am very much aware of that on a conscious level. I don't know why I would dream it."

Therapist: "What else can you tell me about him?"

Client: "Well, he used to be a wealthy man, but he invested all of his money into real estate and now he is trapped and can't leave where he is because of that, and that is why he can't come to visit."

Therapist: "Tell me about your uncle Ed."

Client: "I like him very much too, but he is totally different from my brother-in-law. He really doesn't think about the future at all. He has

spent every cent he ever had, he lives way above his means, and now
he is close to sixty and he has nothing to carry him in his old age."

Therapist: "Do you see any aspects of either of them in yourself?"

Client: "Not really. I am probably more like my brother-in-law than my
uncle Ed."

Therapist: "Neither of them has planned too well for the future. One is
trapped because he overinvested in real estate and the other one because he spent all of his money and didn't save for the future. What
comes to your mind when you think of either being trapped when in-
vesting in real estate or being old and having nothing to show for it?"

Client: "I am thinking of buying a building, and on the one hand, I worry
that I may get trapped with a mortgage; on the other hand, I worry
about growing old and having nothing to my name. I didn't realize that
my brother-in-law and my uncle represented two sides of my conflict."

The following dream was related by a man who was having difficulty
making a decision about which school to choose for his child. He was trying to decide between a religious school and one that the child was already in. He could not understand what his dream was about until he described the persons who were in it.

> *I dreamed that Nina was going to lose all of her valuables, the inheritance that her
> parents had left her, unless she got back with Andrew, her ex-husband. I am very
> worried for her, but she still can salvage what she has if she remarries Andrew.*

Therapist: "Who is Nina?"

Client: "Nina is a good friend of ours. I like her a lot, but she is frequently irresponsible and careless."

Therapist: "Who is Andrew?"

Client: "Andrew is her ex-husband. I haven't seen him in years. I used
to like him very much, but he is kind of irresponsible too. We used to
be very close once. As a matter of fact, he was my child's godfather,
and Nina is his godmother."

Therapist: "What is a godfather?"

Client: "Someone who preserves religious values."

Therapist: "Do you see any relationship between this dream and the decision you are about to make?"

Client: "The dream is telling me not to be irresponsible with my heritage
and to preserve the religious values."

As was noted before, everything in a dream is symbolic, including both
actions and objects. Therefore, a therapist has to interpret every symbol
in the dream. Symbols are very important because they constitute the basis
of the language of dreams. These symbols are used to build a dream story.
Following interpretation of the main symbols in a dream, the therapist

can reconstitute all of the elements and rewrite the dream into its new meaning. The following dream will be used to illustrate how symbols are used to build a dream story and how translation of these symbols can result in a new story. This dream was related by a young woman who had a series of unsatisfactory relationships:

> Les, Matt, Arthur, George and others are in the dream, and we are going to a show. We stop to have something to eat, and I go ahead of them and pay for the pizza. I expect them to pay for their share, but the waiter brings the pizza which is very good and not what I ordered. I am very disappointed, as I was looking forward to it. Then he gives me the change from the money I paid, but it is all foreign currency and nothing that I can use. When I come back from talking to the waiter, they have all gone without me, and I am left alone. I never get to the show.

The general feeling in the dream is one of disappointment and frustration. The dreamer gives to everybody, expecting them to reciprocate, but they don't. What she gets is unsatisfactory, and even when she gets something in return, it is useless. She is left alone and never gets where she wants. This dream was essentially a microcosm of the dreamer's relationships with men. Let us see how defining the symbols and associations to these symbols can further clarify the dream meaning.

The first symbol in the dream is Les, Matt, Arthur, George and others. The client defined these as "my old boyfriends." Her to-the-point association to them was: "men I have liked but who have ended up taking advantage of me." Combining the definition and the to-the-point association suggests that Les, Matt, Arthur, George and others represent the client's previous relationships.

The second symbol in the dream, the show, was defined as "some place you go to at the end of an evening when you are out with a man." She associated this symbol as "something I like very much, something my girlfriends always go to but that somehow my boyfriends don't take me out to." To get at what the show represented, she was asked, "What is something that you have always wanted to get to with men, that all your girlfriends have but that you don't?" The show for her symbolized a committed relationship or marriage.

The client defined the third symbol, pizza, as "something good to eat; nourishment." Her associations to pizza were "something I love and crave but deprive myself of." The question combining the characteristics of the symbol's definition and its associations ("What kind of nourishment do you crave but are deprived of?") elicited the answer "emotional nourishment." Thus, the pizza in this dream was a symbol of the emotional nourishment that the client craved.

The symbol waiter was defined as "someone who serves you with food." Her to-the-point associations to the waiter were, "someone who isn't giving me what I want and what he gives me is totally useless." The combination of the definition and the to-the-point association resulted in the meaning of the symbol. When the client was asked who in her life was giving her nourishment that was unsatisfactory and totally useless, she realized that the waiter represented her current relationship.

When asked for a definition of the symbol of money, the client replied, "Something you give to get what you want." Her associations to this were as follows: "I am very generous. I always pay for everyone, I give it freely to anybody whether they return it or not. I have frequently been taken advantage of." She was asked: "What else do you give freely to others and don't get returns on?" In this case, money represented the energy invested in relationships.

The symbol foreign change was defined as "something you get in return" and associated to as "useless and not what I want, entirely unsatisfactory." When asked what she was getting from her current relationship that was not what she wanted and that was useless and unsatisfactory, it was apparent that the symbol of foreign change stood for the returns she was getting from her current relationship. She wanted marriage, and what she had was a long-distance affair.

As the meaning of the symbols becomes clear, the dream can be rewritten as follows:

> In my previous relationships, I have wanted to get married. I have gone ahead and given emotional nourishment, expecting to have it reciprocated, but that hasn't happened. What my current relationship is giving me is not what I want, and it is unsatisfactory. I have invested a great deal of emotional energy into the relationship, but what I get in return is totally useless. I am also left alone and never get the committed relationship I want.

Let us look at another example of how a dream can be reconstructed into new meaning by interpreting the different symbols in it. A middle-aged woman was attempting to make a decision between going back to an old boyfriend or remaining with her current one. She had the following dream:

> I am in a car with my mother. She is driving the car and keeps stopping on the highway. It is very unsafe. We come to a Y in the road. One road leads to a covered bridge, and the other is a straight road. I think she should go to the straight road, but she wants to go to the covered bridge.

By translating the symbols, the meaning of the dream becomes clear. The first symbol in the dream, that of a car, was defined as "a vehicle that you move about in the world to get you from one place to another." Her direct association to this was that she was usually a good driver and had pretty good control of her car. In answer to the question, "What is the vehicle in which you move about that gets you from one place to another that you are usually in control of?" she stated, "Myself, the way I operate." The car thus symbolized the client's manner of operating.

The symbol mother was defined in this case as "someone who is very passive and dependent and needs to be taken care of; someone who doesn't like to make decisions." Her direct associations were, "My mother in reality doesn't drive. I am not like her at all." When asked if she saw any aspects of her mother in herself, the client felt that her mother in the dream symbolized her passive, indecisive part that wanted to be taken care of.

The client defined a highway as "a road you travel on" and stated that she liked driving on highways, reporting, "I usually drive straight on without stopping and go directly to my destination." The question that combined characteristics of the definition and the direct association to the symbol ("What road are you traveling on that you usually drive without interruption but that you are stopping on now?") elicited the latent meaning of the symbol. The highway stood for the road of life, the road leading to the patient's decision.

The action of stopping represented the client's indecision. Stopping was defined as "to falter" and associated to as being dangerous. "How do you keep stopping or faltering in your current situation?" she was asked. The stopping represented her indecisiveness.

The Y in the road was defined as "a place on the road where you have to make a choice," with the following spontaneous to-the-point association: "It reminds me of my situation now. I must make a decision." The Y in the road represented the decision she needed to make.

The symbol of the covered bridge was defined as "something that links to something else." Her to-the-point association to the bridge was that it looked like the scenery of her past. She was asked, "Which of the roads that you would take is a link to the past that you really don't want to go to but that your passive part wants?" The road leading to the covered bridge represented her past with John.

The client defined the straight road as "a road that leads ahead." She associated to this as follows: "I am not sure where it leads to, but it seems pretty clear the scenery is similar to that of Arizona, my present surroundings." The characteristics of the definition and the to-the-point associations are combined in the following question: "What road lies ahead of you that you are not sure where it will lead to but that has to do with your present?" The straight road represented the future with Lenny, her current boyfriend.

The dream can be reconstructed into the following new dream story:

> I am letting my passive–dependent side that wants to be taken care of make my decision for me. My indecision is dangerous and could destroy my relationship with Lenny. I have come to a point where I must make a decision. The part of me that wants to be taken care of wants to go back to the past with my old boyfriend. The independent part wants to continue my future with Lenny.

CONCLUSION

The combination of defining the symbols and getting the to-the-point associations for them is an effective method for determining the meaning of the symbols and rewriting the dream story. Although this process may seem fairly simple in the above examples, it is easy to get sidetracked during the inquiry, either through the therapist's own associations or through the client's tangentiality. The therapist can stay on track by going back to the common characteristics between symbol and referent. Those shared common characteristics are the link between the latent and manifest meaning of the symbols. Arriving at the new meaning of symbols enables the therapist to interpret the dream and subsequently arrive at the dream message.

Chapter 10
Dream Mechanisms

To dream is nothing else but to think sleeping.
Daniel Defoe, *History of the Devil*

Before discussion of the final steps in interpreting a dream, a chapter on dream mechanisms is included, since these mechanisms intersect across all of the basic steps in the interpretive process. It has already been noted that dream language is like a foreign language and that dream interpretation is translating from one level of consciousness to another. Symbols provide the vocabulary of this new language. Dream mechanisms are the rules of grammar or logic. These rules are very different from the ones followed in everyday logic. An understanding of the syntax of dream language is important in arriving at the dream meaning.

When material is transferred from one level of awareness to another, it is transformed or distorted. The material prior to translation is transformed into new meaning by processes called dream mechanisms. Freud originally named five dream mechanisms, one of which was symbolization. Rosenthal (1980) stated that all of Freud's dream mechanisms were distortions of reality and added 12 other distortions. Some of the common dream mechanisms will be described so that the therapist can recognize them when working with dreams. If the clinician is aware of these characteristics of dream language, it will create less confusion when conducting the interpretive process.

SYMBOLIZATION

One of the primary dream mechanisms, symbolization is the use of concrete symbols to stand for abstract concepts. Both the objects and actions in dreams are symbolic, and dream interpretation consists of translating those symbols into the ideas or objects for which they stand. Symbols are personal to the dreamer, and it is not possible to understand what they refer to without getting the dreamer's associations to them. Symbols share common characteristics with the objects for which they stand, and a

103

description of these common characteristics provides a clue to the meaning of the symbol.

Symbols can stand for objects, actions, or rather complex thoughts. Many of the symbols described in previous chapters generally stood for abstract concepts. For example, a bomb in one case represented an individual's violent temper, a pizza represented emotional nourishment, money represented energy, and so on. Sometimes a symbol can describe a more complex idea. A word or phrase can summarize a combination of ideas. For example, Lillian had a dream that she was to meet the contractor of the building she was buying on Tuesday evening, July the first. She recalled that on that particular date she had invited a speaker to a meeting. The speaker had requested a television so that she could play a videotape that would demonstrate and communicate her ideas more effectively. Although Lillian wanted very much to view this videotape, obtaining a television for the speaker would be more than a minor inconvenience. She would have to make special arrangements for it, carry it, and be responsible for it. In short, it would require some energy. A part of her did not want to be bothered. On the other hand, she was looking forward to hearing this speaker and wondered whether she would get as much from a lecture alone without the accompanying videotape. Before she went to sleep, she debated whether the cost of getting the videotape was worth the advantage of having a good presentation. This complex situation was succinctly summarized in the phrase "Tuesday evening, July 1," which represented a conflict between wanting to have something and wondering whether the costs were worth the effort. By dreaming about meeting the contractor of the building she was about to buy, she conveyed the ambivalence she felt about buying the building, wanting it badly on the one hand and not wanting the inconvenience, on the other.

Both pictures and events can serve as symbols. A picture can convey a particular mood or situation. For example, a picture of a dreamer in a particular city can represent a whole period of his or her life. Occasionally, dreams can consist of a series of pictures or scenes. Somehow the dreamer knows that these scenes are connected or part of the same dream, even though each scene is different from the other. These "serial dreams" —a series of events following another—are common and are the dream's way of conveying a number of ideas that either follow each other or are related to each other in different ways. The juxtaposition of scenes is important, and if we can put in connecting words between one scene and another, the dream makes more sense. For example, Scene 1 could represent the dreamer's current situation, Scene 2 could represent the past where it started, and Scene 3 could depict the future. Scene 1 happened *because of* Scene 2; *therefore*, it leads to Scene 3. For example, Carol had the following "serial dream:"

In the first part of the dream, I am trying to get to a party, but along the way I keep meeting some men who need my help, and I help them, and somehow, I can't seem to make it to the party. I then go to my car but it is stuck, and I can't move it. Then the scene shifts, and I go to the basement of my house and my father is there. Then somehow I am in the car again, and this time the car moves.

The first scene depicted Carol's current situation. She is unable to do something she wants because she is taking care of men's needs first. She is stuck and can't seem to move on. The second scene represents the past and traces the origin of Carol's problem with men to her relationship with her father. The third scene depicts the future and suggests that she can move forward once she deals with the roots of her problem.

There is usually a causal relationship between different scenes, and frequently different time frames are conveyed in the various scenes. Since we cannot dream in the abstract, there is no mechanism for conveying causal elements or relationships. The shifting of scenes conveys this causal connection. Each scene or narrative event can stand for a different idea or represent a specific period in a person's past, present, or future.

Just as causal relationships and complex ideas are difficult to express in a nonabstract medium, so are feelings. Sometimes we use concrete symbols that stand for specific feelings. For example, a tiger that is out of control may represent an individual's anger. Frequently, however, we do not dream about feelings –we *experience* them. We may feel sad, happy, elated, or frustrated in our dreams. Sometimes we wake up with these feelings. A woman hungry for emotional closeness frequently has dreams where she feels famished. A man dealing with the loss of his wife feels very sad in his dreams. The experience of sadness, frustration, hunger, or coldness in dreams is a representation of that feeling in waking life.

Besides the experiencing of feelings to symbolize certain experiences in our waking life, another particular type of symbolization that is characteristic of dream language is that of symbolic metaphor. Since we cannot dream in the abstract, we use concrete pictures to depict specific actions. Some metaphors are fairly obvious, and the words describing the dream picture could be interpreted at several levels. For example, images of opening and shutting doors could represent opening or shutting doors to specific situations, an image of having the right key could mean having the key or solution to a problem, and a picture of oneself in the dark could represent being in the dark or unaware of a specific issue. Other instances of concrete images that may be used to depict abstract actions include being stuck, being on the right track, getting rid of garbage, flying high, not being in the driver's seat, being cut open, being in muddy waters, and so on.

Sometimes images are used to depict specific expressions. These are not as obvious as the ones mentioned above, but the therapist's awareness of their occurrence can help him or her listen for them, particularly if the dreamer's actions in the dream are not immediately understandable at a symbolic level. Examples of images that represent common expressions include dreaming that one is hitting the roof, has egg on one's face, or is having the rug pulled out from under. The dream concretizes these expressions.

Dream language is a clever, creative nonabstract medium for conveying complicated ideas, and visual and verbal metaphor and punning are part of this language. The therapist can listen for these verbal expressions in the telling of the dream. Bonnie, for example, had a dream that made no sense to her until she started relating it. She dreamed that she had an iron in her hands and was ironing her face. As she related the dream, she realized that her picture was a metaphor for "ironing out the wrinkles." Sarah had a dream that she was a chicken locked up in chicken wire. As she told the dream, she realized that she was "chicken" about a specific situation. Harry had a dream in which his wife was very thin, almost sticklike, and was immersed in mud, a "stick-in-the-mud."

Punning is also a characteristic of dream language that therapists should listen for, particularly when a name, word, or phrase occurs that is not easily explained. Bonnie related a dream about a woman named "Careme" (pronounced *care-me*). She recognized that she was dreaming about an aspect of her that needed caring. Another woman dreamed of a man named "Cando" (pronounced *can-do*). This was an image of someone who "can do" something. Sometimes words that sound alike are substituted for other words. For example, a person picturing a "sun" that he is losing may be referring to his "son," or a person picturing someone giving him a "shoe" may be dreaming about someone giving him a "shoo." Being aware of these characteristics of dream language can help the clinician listen for them.

DRAMATIZATION

Another common dream mechanism is dramatization, which is an exaggeration of reality. I have at times referred to this as "absurdization" or "caricature." The very absurdity of the image can serve to poke fun of it and put it in perspective. Bonnie, for example, dreamed of a man with a penis that was so long so as to be ridiculous. This served to dramatize for her the humor in placing so much importance on male qualities. An exaggeration in a dream may be a good focal point; by pointing out the absurdity, it conveys the dream message.

Another dream that has used this dream mechanism was the one related in a previous chapter of a clinical psychologist taking out teeth and pulling out tonsils. That dream highlights the absurdity of the situation in which a person tries to do everything. Humor is an effective way of dealing with neurotic behavior and helps the dreamer have perspective on his or her actions.

Donald also used exaggeration in his dream to help him put his situation in its proper perspective. Donald missed his family and was lonely for them. He dreamed that he was in New York City, and there was not one person in all of New York! The dream not only helped bring to awareness his exaggerated feelings of aloneness, but added humor to the situation.

Sometimes caricatured images elicit the same effect. Linda, for example, dreamed of a woman who was dieting so much that her head was disproportionately big to the rest of her body. This served as a reminder to Linda of her "big-headedness" and the extremes in which she was behaving. Joan dreamed of a man whose head was on backwards. The dream dramatized for her how she always chose "backward" men, men who were occupationally and intellectually inferior to her.

When dramatization or exaggeration is used in dreams, it is frequently a focal point from which to view the rest of the dream, and it usually conveys the dream message through humor. One of the characteristics of dream language is its playful nature.

NUMBERIZATION

Numberization, a term coined by Hattie Rosenthal (1980), refers to numbers occurring in a dream. Numbers can turn out to be a source of valuable information if not the key to a dream message. Rosenthal (1978b) described a rather dramatic example of numbers helping to elucidate the dream message. She had treated a criminal on probation who had bludgeoned a neighbor to death. He had a dream that he was swimming in the ocean and had the feeling that he was sinking. Wherever he turned, a wooden plank would hit him and then another. Although he tried to desperately hold on to them, they would throw him off. These planks seemed to have life in them and hurt him badly. He was furious at them because they were so much stronger than he was. The dreamer did not produce any associations in this dream until he was asked how many planks had attacked him. Without any hesitation, he responded, "Sixteen." He was asked: "How many people are there in your family?" He quickly counted on his fingers and came up with the number sixteen. He was then able to talk about his family and particularly his brother whom he had wanted to murder. In killing his neighbor, he had recreated a fantasy he had about killing his brother. Without the number, further inquiry would likely have produced the same result. However, much time was saved in this manner.

The use of numbers in dreams is no coincidence and usually serves as a characteristic of the objects described. For example, in the dream reported at the beginning of the book, the woman dreamed that three people were being served ahead of her. She had three stepchildren. Whenever clients mention many, several, or a few objects or people, it is generally a good idea to ask for a number, since it often provides a clue to the meaning of the dream.

When numbers are reported spontaneously, they should definitely be noted. Edgar, for example, reported this dream following some career decisions he was trying to make:

> I dreamed that I had done something and had to go to jail for it for thirty years. I was very sad about it but knew that I had to go to jail.

Therapist: "How old will you be in thirty years, Edgar?"
Client: "Sixty-five."
Therapist: "And what happens to people when they turn sixty-five?"
Client: "They retire!"

Through the use of numbers, Edgar realized that his jail term represented the career decision he was contemplating. The dream helped clarify for him his feelings about it. Again, he may have achieved the same insight without the number. The number, however, saved many steps in interpretation and helped him arrive at the dream meaning sooner.

Some time ago, I had a dream in which a certain four-figure number appeared. I could not figure out what those numbers represented, but I vaguely recalled thinking that they reminded me of a telephone extension number. I went to the telephone and dialed the first three digits spontaneously (which were not in the dream, but my unconscious knew what it was doing!) and then the four digits I had dreamed about. It turned out to be the main switchboard number of a place I had worked for and had "forgotten." Numbers in dreams are significant, not coincidental. They can frequently be used as the focal point in interpreting dreams.

CONDENSATION AND DILATION

Condensation is a dream mechanism where several elements are pushed together into one; for example, an uncle may stand for the rest of the family or a co-worker may stand for co-workers in general. It is an economical way to represent ideas in dreams.

Dream language is clever and creative, and frequently several ideas can be condensed into one image or word. For example, a mother of a 5-year-old boy was concerned about his future choice of wife. She had a dream where she asked the mother of Don, an intellectually limited boy, what type of girl he would marry. The mother replied, "A *simple* one, of course", with the emphasis on the word "simple." This condensed two ideas very well: "He's a simple (not bright) boy; he'll marry a simple girl," and "The solution is simple—why are you worrying about your son who is only five now?"

Dilation is the opposite of condensation (Rosenthal, 1980). Whereas in condensation, several objects are condensed into one, in dilation, one issue is spread out into several dimensions in a diffuse, rambling, or repetitive manner. The issue is dilated or spread out so that there is a redundancy.

Jerry's dream is an example of dilation:

> I was trying to get to a party, and on the way, I see two of my colleagues who seem to be having car problems. I fix their car for them and get dirty. They go on but I need to go and wash up before I can go. As I am about to wash up, Diana calls me and asks me if I would mind picking her up on my way. I say I'll do that even though she lives several miles out of the way. However, by the time I get there, she has left a note that she got a ride from someone else. I am upset by that but I figure that as long as I am in her neighborhood I might as well look up some old time friends who live there. I see them at a distance waving at me. They seem to have some problem with their sprinkler system, and I go check it out. I get wet and realize I need a change of clothes. My friends remain dry.

The same theme is repeated over and over here. The dreamer keeps stopping to help others before he meets his own needs. He gets delayed, while they go on their way. The redundancy in the dream seems to highlight the dreamer's pattern.

Condensation and dilation are frequently seen in dreams, and awareness of these mechanisms makes the task of interpretation easier for the clinician.

REVERSAL OF ROLES

Reversing of roles (Rosenthal, 1980) is another type of distortion in dreams. It is the projection of feelings, actions, and behavior that the dreamer has onto another person. Of course, this is a common defense mechanism, particularly when the client is not ready to acknowledge certain feelings in him- or herself. At those times, the client may reverse roles with another person and project those feelings onto that person. When reversal of roles occurs in dreams, it may also serve as a diagnostic tool for the clinician as to the types of defenses that the client may be using. It is also a good vehicle for broaching the topic of those unacceptable feelings with the client. For example, a woman with a drinking problem that had been denied for years dreamed that her best friend was an alcoholic. Projecting these unacceptable feelings onto her friend relieved her from the guilt; however, it served as a means of discussing the problem in psychotherapy. People frequently dream of others being angry and behaving in a harsh and punitive manner toward them. The therapist, recognizing that the client may be very uncomfortable with his or her own anger, may use the dream as a vehicle to help the client become aware of these feelings at a conscious level.

DISSIMILATION

Dissimilation is another dream mechanism added by Rosenthal (1980), which the dreamer uses to gain some distance from his or her unacceptable feelings. Dissimilation is a maneuver that disguises the dreamer or other persons in the dreamer's life. In dreams, some dream figures may appear that the dreamer has no conscious knowledge of but who bear some resemblance to people he or she knows. When reporting a dream, clients often say, "I don't know who that person is, but I feel I know her," or "He is somewhat familiar to me." Frequently, these figures are a disguise of themselves or of the therapist. The therapist can clarify who these figures represent by asking the client to describe them. Statements such as, "She is about your height," or "She has your coloring" may give some clue as to the figure's identity. Sometimes, clients will report, "She reminds me of myself when I was younger," or mention a physical or personality feature that bears some resemblance to themselves or to some important figure in their lives. Dissimilation serves the purpose of providing distance between the dream and what it represents so that the dreamer can decide how much of the dream material he or she wants to bring to conscious awareness.

FUSION AND TRANSFORMATION
OF IMAGES

Fusion and transformation of images occasionally occur in dreams, and awareness of these two characteristics of dream language can help the therapist when a dream image appears confusing. Fusion is the melting of two or more individuals into one unit (Rosenthal, 1980). For example, a dream figure could have several contradictory traits and represent different aspects of the dreamer's personality or aspects of the dreamer merged with another person. A woman related a dream in which the following dream image appeared:

> There was a woman with gray hair, sort of like mine, but she was wearing it in pigtails, like a little girl's. She was carrying a briefcase in one hand and a doll in the other. She was wearing a rather fancy and professional business suit; however, the material was very bright and colorful, like the type you put on children's drapes.

The contrast between the older, businesslike woman, on the one hand, and the childish features, on the other, suggested that the dream figure may be a combination of persons—in this case, the dreamer in her present life and herself as a little girl.

Transformation of images is similar to fusion, in that an image changes during the course of the dream. Several dreams using transformation were already discussed in previous chapters, for example, the babies who turned into chickens or the brother-in-law who became Uncle Ed. Transformation of figures generally embodies several characteristics in the same image. For example, having the brother-in-law who overinvested in real estate turn into the uncle who didn't save is a combination of characteristics of not planning well for one's future. The dream of babies who turned into chickens also embodies two concepts—one of new beginnings and the other of artistic creations. Sometimes when an object transforms into another during the course of the dream, it may reflect emerging or changing attitudes. For example, the "new beginnings" can merge into "artistic creations."

Both fusion and transformation of images are common dream characteristics and part and parcel of everyday dream language. The therapist's awareness of these mechanisms and recognition of them makes the dream appear less confusing and nonsensical.

OMISSION

Omission of material in dreams is significant and should not be ignored. Omission is a mechanism in which certain material is left out of dreams (Rosenthal, 1980). Sometimes, the dreamer calls attention to the omission directly; when the dreamer does not do so, the therapist should be attuned to what is not being said. A client may state, "I recall three rooms, but I know that there was a fourth one," or "I saw a table with only three legs." Examples of omissions have been provided in previous chapters, as in the case of the woman who dreamed that she had three handicaps but could only figure out two of them. Sometimes clients will omit a whole segment of a dream, for example, relating the beginning of a scene, not recalling the middle, and relating the end. Omissions are important, and the therapist should be attuned to what is missing or omitted in a dream. Frequently, the part that is missing can be used as the focal point of the dream.

CONCLUSION

The dream mechanisms or distortions described in this chapter are some of the ones commonly seen in dreams. Recognizing them when they do occur makes the dream appear less nonsensical and confusing. It must be remembered that dream language has its own characteristics and follows its own rules of logic, which are very different from the rules of everyday conscious logic. An understanding of these rules will aid in the process of interpreting the dream message.

Chapter 11

The Dream Message and Therapeutic Applications

We sometimes from dreams pick up some hint worth improving by . . . reflection.

Thomas Jefferson, Letter to
James Monroe, 1823

Every dream provides a message for the dreamer. Whereas Freud saw dreams as wish fulfillment, Rosenthal viewed them as messages. She stated that we can fulfill our wishes in daydreams, and there is no need to do so in dreams. Dreams generally tell us what we don't know or only know at an unconscious level of awareness. Each dream delivers a message from our unconscious to our conscious level of awareness, and the message suggests a remedy. The message comes in unintelligible or disguised form so that the dreamer can decide whether he or she wants to decode the message or push it back, to understand the problem or to keep it hidden from conscious awareness. As James Hall states: "Dreams are mysterious entities, like messages from an unknown friend who is caring but objective. The handwriting and the language are at times obscure, but there is never any doubt as to the underlying concern for our ultimate welfare" (Hall, 1983, p. 117).

Some messages are fairly easy to understand and difficult to ignore. Kathy, for example, had been assigned a project several months in the past but had not started working on it. She had tried to stop thinking about it but kept having recurring dreams that her supervisor was asking her for progress reports on the project! It was hard to ignore the message of her dreams, even though she had consciously avoided thinking about the work she had to do.

Sometimes, the message is conveyed in the theme of the dream, as in the following:

I am at my house, and there are people there. We are having a potluck or something, and there is steak and salad. Someone asks, "Where are all the extras? There are no potatoes, bread and other trimmings." I think to myself, "Why concentrate on what we don't have rather than on what we have? We have the basics." Then I find out that there are extras that I didn't know we had.

The message was expressed rather clearly in this dream: "Concentrate on what you have rather than on what you don't. You have the basics, and you may find out that you have some extra things you weren't aware you had." The message served as a reminder to this client to count her blessings and not to focus on what was lacking.

Here is another dream told by the same woman. Again, the dream message served as a reminder to her of what she needed to do:

I am supposed to make a presentation. I go early to prepare the room for it, and it is a mess. I look for my co-workers to help me, but they are all busy and seem to ignore me. I rush madly to get the projector for the presentation, but it takes much longer than I thought it would, and then I find out someone else has checked it out already. I don't know what to do, and I am worried about being late. I worry about everyone being there and nothing being ready. Then I go back in the room, and everything seems to have taken care of itself. The projector is there, the room was cleaned, and I think to myself that I worried so much over nothing, that in the end everything took care of itself.

As in the previous dream, the message was what the dreamer was telling herself; in this case, "Don't worry so much needlessly. In the long run, everything somehow takes care of itself."

Sometimes the dream message is conveyed through another person, usually someone we respect and admire. Jean had the following dream in which her brother communicated the dream message:

I have a tumble-mat and a cuckoo clock. So does my brother. I worry that the padding on my mat is too thin. His is much thicker. He then whispers something very important to me. He tells me that I have enough padding, that it's adequate, but that I have to be much more careful with it.

Jean had been saving money for a trip, and time was running out before the trip was due (symbolized by the cuckoo clock). She was worried if the money she had saved provided enough of a cushion ("padding") to fall back on ("a tumble-mat is something you fall back on when you play"). The dream message was that her cushion was adequate, but that she would have to be very careful with it. She decided to save some more money so that she would not have to be so careful.

Sometimes the dream message is not communicated so directly and needs to be spelled out. Loren, for example, related the following dream:

I am in a vehicle, and I notice part of my hunk of chain is missing. I need to get it in order to move ahead.

The dream in this case depicted Loren's situation, that he was losing his connections with others, and that in order to get ahead, he needed to make stronger ties. The dream message was for him to start making some connections.

In another dream, Loren had an image of a garage door that he couldn't close because he had too much stuff in it. He related that to his work situation and acted on the dream message to eliminate some of the stuff so that he could close the door.

Occasionally dream messages make clients aware of the progress they are making. Clients frequently dream of themselves behaving in certain ways and contrasting that behavior with their behavior in the past. These progress reports are similar to "appreciation" or "Thank God!" dreams. In appreciation dreams, people may dream of a period of their lives when they were unhappy or when something unfortunate was happening to them. These dreams remind the dreamer to appreciate what he or she has. Harold, for example, frequently dreamed of his adolescence, when he was a shy, unattractive, unpopular teenager. This sharply contrasted with his present circumstances, where he was confident, attractive, and popular with the opposite sex.

"Thank God!" dreams also have as their purpose to bring to the dreamer's awareness what he or she has. Sometimes people have dreams in which they lose a loved one through death or divorce, which is a sharp contrast to the reality of their situation. I have termed these dreams "Thank God!" dreams because a person's immediate reaction upon awakening is "Thank God this didn't happen!" Rather than be upset by these dreams, they can serve as reminders to appreciate what you have.

Dreams give two kinds of messages: what to do or what not to do. A message generally tells the dreamer in which direction to go. Once the dream is analyzed (even if there is not a total interpretation), the therapist should ask, "What do you think the message is?" or "What do you think the dream is telling you?"

Dreams have both diagnostic and therapeutic applications. Once the dreamer understands his or her behavior, the next step is to apply the dream message to his or her life; otherwise, the entire interpretation would go to waste. The most important part of therapy is what the client does with the self-knowledge. Once the dream interpretation is finished and the client is able to verbalize the dream message, the therapist can ask: "How can you use this self-knowledge?" or "How can you apply this to yourself?" This is very important. Both the *diagnostic* and the *therapeutic* aspects are necessary in dream analysis. Interpreting the dream is only part of the process; the practical application of its message completes it.

Let us see how that might work by looking at some of the dreams discussed in this chapter where the dream message was elicited. Kathy, for example, whose dreams were telling her to work on her project, could easily apply this to her life by discussing with her therapist why she was procrastinating and then setting up a schedule to work on her project. In this case, the dream was quite helpful, since it elicited a long discussion of Kathy's fear of failure and some of her poor organizational skills. The therapist was able to provide concrete, helpful, and practical suggestions for completing the project.

The woman who had a dream about concentrating on what she has rather than on what she doesn't could be asked in what situations she can apply this. The client may mention that she tends to complain that she doesn't have money for "extras," but that she really has the basics—food, shelter, clothing—and that she also has some extras of which she isn't aware. She can remind herself of this dream when she finds herself depressed and complaining about her financial situation. She can also be taught some specific thought-stopping and cognitive restructuring techniques to change her thinking. In her second dream, where she was telling herself not to worry so much, she can also be taught some strategies to worry less, for example, by changing her thinking about a situation or by specific relaxation techniques. Once a dream is interpreted, the therapist can use other therapeutic tools to help the client learn practical ways of applying the dream message to his or her life.

Each message in the dream provides a solution. The dreamer can choose to act on the solution or ignore it. Sometimes, it is easier to work out the solution symbolically, *within the dream*, and later apply it to the client's life. This may be less threatening, and the dreamer can see the solutions more clearly. We have seen an example of this in Chapter 6, where the woman was able to figure out what she could do to get better service in the restaurant. She could later apply this solution to her situation with her husband. Most dreams provide obvious solutions to a dilemma, which the client can come up with alone. For example, if the dreamer has a dream that she feels she is out of control because she is driving from the back seat, she can be asked, "What is the obvious solution here?" She can then state, "To get in the driver's seat!" The therapist and client can then discuss specific, concrete situations as to how this can be done.

Sometimes, the therapist can suggest practical applications to use in a later dream. For example, Betty had a recurring nightmare in which she came face to face with her mother. Betty always woke up perspiring from the dream and feeling terrified. It was suggested to her that she confront her mother in the next dream and ask what she wanted from her. This was very effective, in that when she had this dream again, she talked to her mother and told her to leave her alone.

As noted before, the therapist can use any therapeutic modality he or she is comfortable with to work on the dream message. Psychotherapists with a behavioral orientation can use a number of behavioral strategies to change a client's behavior. Gestalt therapists may choose some specific experiential techniques to help their clients act out and experience their conflicts. Some therapists may combine hypnosis with dream analysis. For example, a client can be put into a hypnotic trance in order to re-experience the dream and fill in missing elements. This is particularly helpful when there are omissions reported. Much of the interpretation can then be done metaphorically in a hypnotic state, and the therapist can provide some posthypnotic suggestions on applying the dream message. The possibilities for working with a dream once it is interpreted are numerous and left to the therapist's creativity. It is not the purpose of this book to suggest methods of applying the dream message. These possibilities are only mentioned to reinforce that this method of dream interpretation is compatible with any number of theoretical orientations and can be combined with them.

CONCLUSION

Dreams have both diagnostic and therapeutic applications. Each dream has a message that, once understood, the dreamer can choose to act upon. The therapist can help the client elicit the dream message and apply it practically to his or her life. Each message provides a solution, and sometimes the client can work out the solution at a symbolic level before applying it to his or her life. The practical application of the dream is extremely important and can be adapted to the therapist's psychotherapeutic orientation.

Chapter 12
Summarizing the Interpretive Process

In the previous chapters, we have looked at each of the stages involved in interpreting a dream. In this chapter, these steps will be summarized and illustrated so that we can integrate them and see how they work together in the interpretive process. It must be remembered that dream analysis is a joint venture between therapist and client; a therapist cannot interpret a dream alone, since it is the client who provides the definitions and associations.

Let us look at this dream told by a young woman who originally came for therapy because of test anxiety. She was trying to decide which college to go to at this point and was told to have a dream:

My parents asked each of us to choose a dog and a record album we would like. All my siblings chose except me. I couldn't decide and ended up with nothing. I thought of getting a golden retriever but Michael, my brother, had already chosen one.

1. To *define the pattern*, the therapist can ask the dreamer to tell this as though it were a story, happening to someone else. The client stated, "A woman is trying to choose something. All of her siblings can make a decision except her. She ends up with nothing." The dreamer's pattern of indecision is fairly clear in this dream. By hesitating, she ends up with nothing. She also doesn't get something she likes because her brother chose it first. The client can be asked if she sees any similarity between the dreamer's actions and her own. She related that she found it very difficult to make decisions in general, usually waiting until the last minute to make one. She also felt that she was the only one in her family who did not excel at something. She felt that this dream related to her indecision about which college to go to and consequent career choice. She was the only sibling in her family who had not made a definitive career choice.

2. The therapist can find a *focal point* by asking, "What interests you most in this dream?" or "What is not clear in this dream?" Both the therapist and client chose the record album as a focal point in this case, al-

though inquiry could have started with any of the other symbols in this dream.

3. The therapist can then ask for *definitions* and *to-the-point associations* for each symbol in order to rewrite the dream story. The client gave the following definitions and associations to the symbols. She related that she had a gift certificate for a record album with an expiration date for last week. She had, as usual, waited until the last minute to get it. The album symbolized a deadline and the client's making last minute decisions based on deadlines rather than logic. She said that dogs were something she liked and that she deprived herself of because her brother had gotten there first. When asked what else she liked that she deprived herself of because her brother was there first, she related chemistry. Every one of her siblings excelled in an area except for her. Her brother was first in chemistry and made wonderful grades. She was afraid to major in chemistry for fear of competing with him. The dream started to shed some light on the dreamer's difficulty in deciding which college to go to or which career choice to make. The underlying fear behind her indecisiveness was her fear of failure and competing with her siblings, particularly her brother.

4. The *dream can be rewritten* as follows: "I am having difficulty making a decision about which career choice to make. Each of my siblings has made a career choice and has excelled in something except me. When I make a decision, it is only because there is a deadline and not due to logic. When I hesitate and don't decide, I end up with nothing. I would like to study chemistry, but I am afraid to compete with my brother Michael, because he is first in it."

5. To get at the *message*, the client can be asked, "What do you think this dream is telling you?" or "What do you think the message of the dream is for you?" This client stated, "The dream is telling me not to be afraid to compete or make a wrong decision. Otherwise, I might end up with nothing."

6. The last step is *therapeutic application* of the message. She was asked, "What have you learned about yourself?" She answered, "That I am afraid of competing and failing." The therapist can then ask, "And what can you do with what you have learned?" or "How can you apply this to yourself?" These are questions asking for specific behavior. She responded that she would enroll in the college where she could major in chemistry, even if it might mean she would fail or not do as well as her brother. The client was also asked in what other areas of her life she could apply what she had learned about herself. She responded that she would try to make other decisions even if they were wrong ones rather than wait and end up with nothing.

The preceding discussion illustrates how the process of dream interpretation works in therapy. The steps do not necessarily have to be in the order described or as mechanical as these examples imply. Each client and dream is individual, and each dream analyst in the end has to interview in the manner that is most compatible with his or her style. However, the steps can serve as guidelines for the psychotherapist.

The following is from Hattie Rosenthal's writings (1980, p. 56):

> A few hints can be given in this context which will offer an opening key to the analyzing therapist.
>
> 1. Let the dreamer "generalize" the dream content in an impersonal way and then deduct from the general to the personal meaning.
>
> 2. Let the dreamer repeat the dream as if it were a story he has heard. Then ask in which way his response to the story relates to himself.
>
> 3. Ask him about the mood (psychic climate) displayed in the dream and whether he sees a similarity between the dream mood and his conscious frame of mind.
>
> 4. Sometimes the focal point can be used as an inception.
>
> 5. Let the patient define every symbol used in the dream.
>
> 6. Let the patient find as many answers and to-the-point associations as possible.
>
> 7. Then compose all the dream elements offered by going through the dream step by step.
>
> 8. Help him elicit the dream message.

Two points about dream interpretation that were already made in previous chapters need to be re-emphasized. The first point stressed the importance of being thorough in dream analysis and not overlooking dream details. Every detail is relevant, no matter how unimportant it may appear at first glance—*otherwise we would not dream it.* Frequently, the essence of a dream may be hidden in what appears to be an insignificant detail. Understanding can only be achieved if each portion of the dream is given full attention. The therapist should not let anything go in dream analysis. The more accurate, detailed, and extensive the analysis is, the more the client gets out of a dream. This will save time in the long run.

The second point also has to do with thorough interpretation. If the therapist cannot interpret every element in a dream, it is better to leave the dream partly interpreted than to prematurely and superficially interpret it. Even if the therapist can only interpret part of a dream, the dreamer often gets something out of it. People frequently find the missing pieces to incomplete dreams in later sessions. Sometimes the therapist may suggest to the client to have a dream about what is still unexplained.

How does a therapist begin doing dream analysis? One way to begin is by recording one's dreams and using the above-mentioned steps on oneself. Of course, this is difficult to do unless one does it in writing, but even then one's associations and responses can be illuminating. A more effective way would be to have another person, whether colleague or therapist, serve as the interviewer. Both of these methods give the therapist a "feel" for the process firsthand. The therapist can also ask clients to bring in their dreams and interpret them together using the guidelines presented in this book. As therapists start using these concepts, they are frequently surprised at how much they do get out of a dream. They also learn where they need more practice and can work on the steps that give them the most difficulty. The therapist need not become discouraged if he or she cannot interpret all of a dream or experiences difficulty and confusion at first. It must be remembered that even if one only arrives at the general meaning of a dream, the client gets something from it. As with any other therapeutic tool, practice and experience will increase the therapist's comfort and confidence and help him or her appreciate this valuable tool.

References

Aserinsky, E., & Kleitman, N. (1953). Regularly occurring periods of eye mobility and concomitant phenomena during sleep. *Science, 118,* 273–274.

Beck, A. T., & Ward, C. H. (1961). Dreams of depressed patients: Characteristic themes in manifest content. *Archives of General Psychiatry, 5,* 462–467.

Belicki, K., & Bowers, P. (1982). The role of demand characteristics and hypnotic ability in dream change following a presleep instruction. *Journal of Abnormal Psychology, 91*(6), 426–432.

Breger, L., Hunter, I., & Lane, R. W. (1971). The effect of stress on dreams. *Psychological Issues, 7*(27).

Bressler, B., & Mizrachi, N. (1978a). The first dream as a psychodiagnostic tool: Its use by the primary physician with his psychosomatic patients. *Journal of Asthma Research, 15*(4), 179–189.

Bressler, B., & Mizrachi, N. (1978b). The first dream as a psychodiagnostic tool: II. Parameters. *Journal of Asthma Research, 16*(1), 1–14.

Bynum, E. (1980). The use of dreams in family therapy. *Psychotherapy: Theory, Research and Practice, 17*(2), 227–231.

Cartwright, R. D. (1974a). Problem solving: Waking and dreaming. *Journal of Abnormal Psychology, 83,* 451–455.

Cartwright, R. D. (1974b). The influence of a conscious wish on dreams. *Journal of Abnormal Psychology, 83,* 451–455.

Cartwright, R. D. (1978). *A primer on sleep and dreaming.* Reading, MA: Addison-Wesley.

Cartwright, R. D., Lloyd, S., Knight, S., & Trenholme, I. (1984). Broken dreams: A study of the effects of divorce and depression on dream content. *Psychiatry, 47*(3), 251–259.

Cartwright, R. D., Tipton, L. W., & Wicklund, J. (1980). Focusing on dreams: A preparation program for psychotherapy. *Archives of General Psychiatry, 37*(3), 275–277.

Cavenar, J. O., & Nash, J. L. (1976). The dream as a signal for termination. *Journal of the American Psychoanalytic Association, 24*(2), 425–436.

Cavenar, J. O., & Spaulding, J. G. (1978). Termination signal dreams in psychoanalytic psychotherapy. *Bulletin of The Menninger Clinic, 42*(1), 58–62.

Cirincione, D., Hart, J., Karle, W., & Switzer, A. (1980). The functional approach to using dreams in marital and family therapy. *Journal of Marital and Family Therapy, 6*(2), 147–151.

Crick, F., & Mitchison, G. (1983). The function of dream sleep. *Nature, 304,* 111–114.

Delaney, G. (1979). *Living your dreams.* San Francisco: Harper & Row.

Delaney, G. (1985). *Creative problem-solving in sleep and dreams: Professional creations and personal insights.* Paper presented at the Second Annual Conference for the Association for the Study of Dreams, Charlottesville, VA.

Dement, W. C. (1960). The effect of dream deprivation. *Science, 131,* 1705–1707.

Dement, W. (1964). Experimental dream studies. In *Academy of psychoanalysis: Science and psychoanalysis* (Vol. 7, pp. 129–184). New York: Grune & Stratton.

Dement, W., & Kleitman, N. (1957a). The relation of eye movements during sleep to dream activity: An objective method for the study of dreaming. *Journal of Experimental Psychology, 53*, 339–346.

Dement, W., & Kleitman, N. (1957b). Cyclic variations in EEG during sleep and their relation to eye movements, body motility and dreaming. *Electroencephalography and Clinical Neurophysiology, 9*, 673–690.

Doweiko, H. E. (1982). Neurobiology and dream theory: A rapprochement model. *Individual Psychology: Journal of Adlerian Theory, Research and Practice, 38*(1), 55–61.

Doyle, M. C. (1984). Enhancing dream pleasure with Senoi strategy. *Journal of Clinical Psychology, 40*(2), 467–474.

Evans, C. (1983). *Landscapes of the night: How and why we dream.* New York: Viking.

Faraday, A. (1972). *Dream power.* New York: Coward, McCann & Geoghegan.

Faraday, A. (1974). *The dream game.* New York: Harper & Row.

Fiss, H. (1983). Toward a clinically relevant experimental psychology of dreaming. *Hillside Journal of Clinical Psychiatry, 5*(2), 147–159.

Fiss, H., Klein, G. S., & Shollar, E. (1974). "Dream intensification" as a function of prolonged REM period interruption. *Psychoanalysis and Contemporary Science, 3*, 399–424.

Fiss, H., & Litchman, J. (1976). *"Dream enhancement": An experimental approach to the adaptive function of dreams.* Paper presented at the Association for the Psychophysiological Study of Sleep, Cincinnati, OH.

Fleiss, R. (1953). *The revival of interest in the dream.* New York: International Universities Press.

Fosshage, J. L. (1983). The psychological function of dreams: A revised psychoanalytic perspective. *Psychoanalysis and Contemporary Thought, 6*(4), 641–669.

Foulkes, D. (1962). Dream reports from different stages of sleep. *Journal of Abnormal and Social Psychology, 65*, 14–28.

Foulkes, D., & Rechtschaffen, A. (1964). Presleep determinants of dream content: Effects of two films. *Perceptual and Motor Skills, 19*, 983–1005.

French, T. M., & Fromm, E. (1964). *Dream interpretation: A new approach.* New York: Basic Books.

Freud, S. (1950). *The interpretation of dreams.* New York: Random House.

Garfield, P. (1974). *Creative dreaming.* New York: Ballantine.

Garfield, P. (1984). *Your child's dreams.* New York: Ballantine.

Gillin, C., & Wyatt, R. (1975). Schizophrenia: Perchance a dream. *International Review of Neurobiology, 17*, 297–342.

Gold, L. (1979). Adler's theory of dreams: An holistic approach to interpretation. In B. B. Wolman (Ed.), *Handbook of dreams* (pp. 319–341). New York: Van Nostrand Reinhold.

Goldstein, A. P., & Dean, S. J. (Eds.). (1966). *The investigation of psychotherapy.* New York: John Wiley & Sons.

Greenberg, R., Pillard, R., & Pearlman, C. (1972). The effect of dream (stage REM) deprivation on adaptation to stress. *Psychosomatic Medicine, 34*, 257–262.

Greene, T. A. (1979). C. G. Jung's theory of dreams. In Wolman, B. B. (Ed.), *Handbook of dreams* (pp. 298–318). New York: Van Nostrand Reinhold.

Greiser, C., Greenberg, R., & Harrison, R. (1972). The adaptive function of sleep. *Journal of Abnormal Psychology, 80*, 280–286.

Hall, C. S. (1947). Diagnosing personality by the analysis of dreams. *Journal of Abnormal and Social Psychology, 42*, 68–79.

Hall, C. S. (1953). *The meaning of dreams.* New York: Harper and Brothers.

Hall, C. S., & Domhoff, B. (1963). A ubiquitous sex difference in dreams. *Journal of Abnormal and Social Psychology, 66*, 278–280.

Hall, C. S., & Van de Castle, R. L. (1966). *The content analysis of dreams.* New York: Appleton-Century Crofts.

Hall, J. A. (1983). *Jungian dream interpretation*. Toronto: Inner City Books.

Hall, J. A. (1984). Dreams and transference/countertransference: The transformative field. *Chiron*, 31–51.

Hauri, P. (1976). Dreams in patients remitted from reactive depression. *Journal of Abnormal Psychology, 85*, 1–10.

Himelstein, P. (1984). Dream symbol or dream process? *Psychology: A Quarterly Journal of Human Behavior, 21*(1), 9–11.

Hobson, J. A., & McCarley, R. W. (1977). The brain as a dream state generator: An activation-synthesis hypothesis of the dream process. *American Journal of Psychiatry, 134*, 1335–1348.

Jacobs, E. (1982). Dream theatre: Working from children's dreams. *Dreamworks, 3*(1), 7–9.

Jokipaltio, L. (1982). Dreams in child psychoanalysis. *Scandinavian Psychoanalytic Review, 5*(1), 31–47.

Jones, R. M. (1968). The psychoanalytic theory of dreaming. *Journal of Nervous and Mental Disease, 147*(6), 587–603.

Jones, R. M. (1970). *The new psychology of dreaming*. New York: Grune & Stratton.

Jung, C. G. (Ed.). (1964). *Man and his symbols*. New York: Dell.

Kaplan, J., Saayman, G., & Faber, P. A. (1981). An investigation of the use of nocturnal dream reports as diagnostic indices in the assessment of family problem solving. *Journal of Family Therapy, 3*(3), 227–242.

Koch-Sheras, P. E. (1985). *A re-examination of the difference between men's and women's dreams*. Paper presented at the Second Annual International Conference of the Association for the Study of Dreams, Charlottesville, VA.

Kramer, M., Hlasny, R., Jacobs, G., & Roth, T. (1976). Do dreams have meaning? An empirical inquiry. *American Journal of Psychiatry, 133*, 778–781.

Kramer, M., Whitman, R. M., Baldridge, B., & Lansky, L. (1966). Dreaming in the depressed. *Canadian Psychiatric Association Journal, 11*, 178–192.

Kramer, M., Whitman, R. M., Baldridge, B., & Ornstein, P. H. (1968). Drugs and dreams III. The effects of imipramine on the dreams of depressed patients. *American Journal of Psychiatry, 124*, 1385–1392.

Kramer, M., Whitman, R. M., Baldridge, B., & Ornstein, P. H. (1970). Dream content in male schizophrenic patients. *Diseases of the Nervous System, 31*, 51–58.

Krohn, A. (1972). *Levels of object representations in the manifest dreams and projective tests*. Unpublished doctoral dissertation, University of Michigan.

Krohn, A., & Mayman, M. (1974). Object representations in dreams and projective tests: A construct validational study. *Bulletin of the Menninger Clinic, 38*, 445–466.

Labruzza, A. L. (1978). The activation-synthesis hypothesis of dreams: A theoretical note. *American Journal of Psychiatry, 135*(12), 1536–1538.

Langs, R. (1966). Manifest dreams from three clinical groups. *Archives of General Psychiatry, 14*, 634–643.

Langs, R. (1982). Supervisory crises and dreams from supervisees. *Contemporary Psychoanalysis, 18*(4), 575–612.

Levay, A. N., & Weissberg, J. (1979). The role of dreams in sex therapy. *Journal of Sex and Marital Therapy, 5*(4), 334–339.

LeVine, R. (1966). *Dreams and deeds: Achievement motivation in Nigeria*. Chicago: University of Chicago Press.

Lewin, I., & Glaubman, H. (1975). The effect of REM deprivation: Is it detrimental, beneficial, or neutral? *Psychophysiology, 12*, 349–353.

Makarić, E. (1979). Importance of dreams of alcoholics in their treatment and abstinence. *Socijalna Psihijatrija, 7*(1), 41–53.

Marriott, J. (1980). The non-directive state of hypnosis and subsequent dream-work in resolving a long-standing fear/anxiety state: A case study. *Australian Journal of Clinical Hypnotherapy, 1*(1), 12-16.

Martin, J. (1982). The analyst in the dream: A reappraisal. *Journal Council for the Advancement of Psychoanalytic Education, 2*(2), 43-47.

McCarley, R. W., & Hobson, J. A. (1977). The neurobiological origins of psychoanalytic dream theory. *American Journal of Psychiatry, 134,* 1121-1221.

Merrill, S., & Cary, G. L. (1975). Dream analysis in brief psychotherapy. *American Journal of Psychotherapy, 29,* 185-192.

Miller, J. B. (1969). Dreams during various stages of depression. *Archives of General Psychiatry, 20,* 560-565.

Miller, M. J., Stinson, L. W., & Soper, B. (1982). The use of dream discussions in counseling. *Personnel and Guidance Journal, 61*(3), 142-145.

Mindell, A. (1982). *Dreambody.* Boston: Sigo Press.

Offenkrantz, W., & Rechtschaffen, A. (1963). Clinical studies of sequential dreams. *Archives of General Psychiatry, 8,* 497-508.

Okuma, T., Sunami, Y., Fukuma, E., Takeo, S., & Motoike, M. (1970). Dream content study in chronic schizophrenics and normals by REMP-awakening techniques. *Folia Psychiatrica et Neurologica Japonica, 3,* 151-162.

Palombo, S. R. (1984). Recovery of early memories associated with reported dream imagery. *American Journal of Psychiatry, 141*(12), 1508-1511.

Perlmutter, R. A., & Babineau, R. (1983). The use of dreams in couples therapy. *Psychiatry, 46*(1), 66-72.

Perls, F. S. (1969). *Gestalt therapy verbatim.* Lafayette, CA: Real People Press.

Rechtschaffen, A., Verdone, P., & Wheaton, J. (1963). Reports of mental activity during sleep. *Canadian Psychiatric Association Journal, 8,* 409-414.

Reiser, M. F. (1984). *Mind, brain, body: Toward a convergence of psychoanalysis and neurobiology.* New York: Basic Books.

Reitav, J. (1985). *Psychological defenses and the prediction of dream recall failure.* Paper presented at the Second Annual International Conference of the Association for the Study of Dreams, Charlottesville, VA.

Roll, S., Hinton, R., & Glazer, M. (1974). Dreams and death: Mexican Americans vs. Anglo-Americans. *Interamerican Journal of Psychology, 8,* 111-115.

Rosenthal, H. R. (1978a). *Against all odds.* Unpublished manuscript.

Rosenthal, H. R. (1978b). A clinical note on the manifest content of dreams. *Modern Psychoanalysis, 2*(2), 228-243.

Rosenthal, H. R. (1980). *The discovery of the sub-unconscious in a new approach to dream analysis.* South Miami, FL: Banyan Books.

Rossi, E. (1972). *Dreams and the growth of personality.* New York: Pergamon Press.

Sarlin, M. B. (1984). The use of dreams in psychotherapy with deaf patients. *Journal of the American Academy of Psychoanalysis, 12*(1), 75-88.

Schonbar, R. A. (1961). Temporal and emotional factors in the selective recall of dreams. *Journal of Consulting Psychology, 25*(1), 67-73.

Scott, J. A. (1982). The principles of rapid dream analysis. *Medical Hypnoanalysis, 3*(3), 85-95.

Spero, M. H. (1984). A psychotherapist's reflections on a countertransference dream. *American Journal of Psychoanalysis, 44*(2), 191-196.

Tihansky, T. (1982). Case report: Mixed arthritis. *Medical Hypnoanalysis, 3*(3), 118-120.

Trosman, H. (1963). Dream research and the psychoanalytic theory of dreams. *Archives of General Psychiatry, 9,* 9-18.

Ullman, M., & Zimmerman, N. (1979). *Working with dreams.* Los Angeles: Jeremy P. Tarcher, Inc.

Van Bork, J. J. (1982). An attempt to clarify a dream-mechanism: Why do people wake up out of an anxiety dream? *International Review of Psychoanalysis, 9*(3), 233–277.

Van de Castle, R. L., & Holloway, J. (1971). Dreams of depressed patients, nondepressed patients, and normals. *Psychophysiology, 7,* 326.

Vogel, G. W. (1978). An alternative view of the neurobiology of dreaming. *American Journal of Psychiatry, 135*(12), 1531–1535.

Warnes, H. (1982). The dream specimen in psychosomatic medicine in the light of clinical observations. *Psychotherapy and Psychosomatics, 38*(1–4), 154–164.

Webb, W. B., & Cartwright, R. D. (1978). Sleep and dreams. *Annual Review of Psychology, 29,* 223–252.

Werman, D. S. (1978). The use of dreams in psychotherapy: Practical guidelines. *Canadian Psychiatric Association Journal, 23*(3), 153–158.

Whitman, R., Kramer, M., & Baldridge, B. (1963). Which dream does the patient tell? *Archives of General Psychiatry, 8,* 277–282.

Winget, C., & Kapp, F. (1972). The relationship of the manifest content of dreams to duration of childbirth in primiparae. *Psychosomatic Medicine, 34*(2), 313–320.

Winget, C., Kramer, M., & Whitman, R. (1972). Dreams and demograpy. *Canadian Psychiatric Association Journal, 17,* 203–208.

Winson, J. (1985). *Brain and psyche.* New York: Doubleday.

Witkin, H. A., & Lewis, H. B. (1967). Presleep experiences and dreams. In H. A. Witkin & H. B. Lewis (Eds.), *Experimental studies of dreaming* (pp. 148–201). New York: Random House.

Zarcone, V., Gulevich, G., Pivik, T., & Dement, W. (1968). Partial REM phase deprivation and schizophrenia. *Archives of General Psychiatry, 18,* 194–202.

Author Index

Subject Index

Dreams (*continued*)
  mechanisms of, 103–111
  message of, 76–77, 81, 112–116, 118
  neurobiology of, 8
  nonpsychological theories of, 8–12
  numberization in, 107–108
  omission of, 111
  problem-solving functions of, 4–5
  process of interpretation, 70–77
  as projections of inner dynamics, 20–21
  psychological theories of, 1–8
  and psychotherapy, 37–50
  psychotherapy applications, 12–17
  and psychotherapy research, 18–36
  psychotherapy studies of, 33–36
  and quality of profound honesty, 52
  recall of, 60
  recording of, 60–63, 76, 80, 100, 118
  as reflections of personality, 19–24
  role reversal during, 109–110
  sexual nature of, 3
  supervisor/supervisee relationships, 17
  theory of, 51–58
  therapeutic applications of, 39, 112–116
  to-the-point associations of, 92–102
  and unique situations, 23–24
  and wish-fulfillment, 3, 53–54
Dreams and the Growth of Personality, 7
Dream Theatre, 16
D State, 8, 19

Enhancement, 27–28
Explanation of dreams, 93

Family therapy, 14–15, 34
Fear, 66
Forgetting, 29
Free-floating association, 2, 93
Freud, Sigmund, 1–17, 29–30, 37, 52, 55, 103
Fromm-Reichman, Freida, viii
FTG cells, 8
Fusion, 110–111

Gestalt theory, 13, 77
Gestalt therapy, 5–6
Group therapy, 14

Hypnoanalysis, 33
Hypnotic Dreams, 12
Images, 105–106
Image transformation, 110–111
Integration, 6
Interpretation, 4, 70–77, 117–120
Interpretation of Dreams, The, 1
Interviewing method, 92–93

Jungian theory, 3–4, 37

Language, 54, 56, 106, 108–109
Latent dream, 1, 7–8, 54
Living Your Dreams, 7, 60

Manifest dream, 1, 7–8, 54
Marital therapy, 14–15
Meaning of Dreams, The, 21
Men
  dreams compared to women's, 22–23
Mind, Brain, Body: Toward a Convergence of Psychoanalysis and Neurobiology, 10–11

Neurobiology, 8
Neuronal units, 8
New Psychology of Dreaming, The, 5
Nodal points, 11
Numberization, 107–108

Omission, 111

Patient
  presentation of dream analysis to, 59–69
Pattern, 73–74, 78–85
  definition of, 117
Perls, Fritz, 5–6
Primer on Sleep and Dreaming, A, 28
Psychoanalysis, 13
  use of dreams in, 37–50
Psychology

dream theories of, 1–8
experimental studies of dreams,
    28–32
Psychosomatic illness, 15
Psychosynthesis, 7
Psychotherapy, 13, 25–26, 34
    with deaf patients, 33
    dream applications, 12–17
    and dream research, 18–36
    studies on the use of dreams, 33–36
Punning, 106

Rapid eye movement (REM), 10–12,
    18–19, 26–28
Recall, 60
REM. See Rapid eye movement
Repression, 30
Resistance, 29, 64–66
Revival of Interest in the Dream, The, 3
Role reversal, 109–110
Rosenthal, Hattie R. Institute, viii

Secondary elaboration, 2
Self-awareness
    development of, 13
Sensitivity-therapy group, 35
Series, 20
Sex, 3
Sex therapy, 14
Sleep, 10–12
    See also Rapid eye movement

Sleep laboratory, 35
Symbolization, 2, 3, 55, 57, 74–76, 99,
    103–106, 118

Therapist
    presentation of dream analysis to
        the patient, 59–69
    and process of dream interpreta-
        tion, 70–77
Therapy
    application of dreams in, 112–116, 118
    family, 14–15, 34
    Gestalt, 5–6
    marital, 14–15
    progress of, 34–35
    sensitivity-group, 35
    sex, 14
Transference, 16–17

Unconscious, 2, 37, 54

Waking behavior
    effect of dreams on, 26–28
Waking conditions
    effect of on dreams, 24–26
Wish-fulfillment, 3, 53–54
Women
    dream comparison to men's, 22–23
Working with Dreams, 14

Your Child's Dreams, 16

About the Author

Lillie Weiss received her doctorate from the State University of New York at Buffalo in 1968. A clinical psychologist in private practice, she co-directs the Center for Psychotherapy and Dream Analysis in Phoenix, Arizona, and is Adjunct Associate Professor in the Department of Psychology at Arizona State University. She is a co-author of *Treating Bulimia: A Psychoeducational Approach* and *You Can't Have Your Cake and Eat It Too: A Program for Controlling Bulimia*.

Psychology Practitioner Guidebooks

Editors
Arnold P. Goldstein, Syracuse University
Leonard Krasner, SUNY at Stony Brook
Sol L. Garfield, Washington University